scientifica
PRESENTS
REESE CYCLE and BENSON BURNER
IN
PEOPLE LIKE US

Louise Petheram

T

Published in 2005 by:
Nelson Thornes Ltd
Delta Place
27 Bath Road
CHELTENHAM
GL53 7TH
United Kingdom

05 06 07 08 09 / 10 9 8 7 6 5 4 3 2 1

A catalogue record for this book is available from the British Library

ISBN 0 7487 9015 2

Cover illustration by Gary Andrews
Illustrations by Oxford Designers and Illustrators
Flick strip illustrations by Darren Watts
Talking heads illustrations by Mark Draisey Limited
Design and page make-up by Darren Watts

Printed and bound in Great Britain by Scotprint

Contents

Introduction

People Like Us is one of three science readers that you can use with the *Scientifica* books. All the articles in *People Like Us* are linked to science topics that you will cover in the *Scientifica* Year 9 book. The Contents page shows you which Unit in the *Scientifica* book each article links to. The articles focus on the way scientists today use creative thinking, experimentation and science knowledge to solve a wide range of different problems.

The articles are ideal to help you with the 'Ideas and Evidence' part of your science course. You will find out how scientists work today, making discoveries or changing scientific ideas into really useful products for industry, medicine or the developing world, for example. You will discover some of the many things we can do with science when we take it 'out of the classroom' and use it to solve a wide range of practical problems.

A 'Questions' section at the end of each article lets you check how well you understood the article. Another section called 'Activities' suggests topics that you can discuss with other students, or ideas you can use to help you find out or understand more about the article you have just read. Sometimes there will be opportunities to talk about how science can really change people's lives, for better or worse, and to discuss whether new developments are a good idea or not.

As you look through *People Like Us* you will see the page numbers are in different colours. This is because the articles are written in three slightly different reading styles; the style of the red pages is slightly harder to read, and the style of the green pages is slightly easier, so you can choose the topic and the reading style that you like best.

Information for teachers

The articles in *People Like Us* all link to topics covered in the Year 9 Programme of Study from the QCA Scheme of Work. They are written at a conceptual level appropriate for Year 9 students, and, within each Unit, the articles provide progression by reading age. *People Like Us* is ideal for the 'Ideas and Evidence' part of your programme of study, supporting development of all the relevant Scientific Enquiry skills needed.

On the most simple level, a 'Questions' section at the end of each article allows you to check students' understanding of the article. On a more complex level, the 'Activities' section allows students to explore, through discussion, research and role-play, their responses to issues raised, and their opinions about how, when and why science discoveries should be used, often linking with Citizenship issues.

There are three articles linking to each QCA Unit in the Scheme of Work, covering different topics, allowing pupils to read different articles and then report back to the class, if you wish.

Choosing your new puppy

Setting the scene

You know that offspring inherit characteristics from their parents. They end up a bit like both parents, but not exactly the same as either parent. You have probably learned that farmers can use selective breeding to breed animals with the characteristics they want, such as hens that lay lots of eggs, or sheep that grow really good-quality wool. But does anyone else use selective breeding, and how well does it work?

Harpreet's family wants to buy a puppy. They have never owned a dog before and they are finding it difficult to choose. They know that there are lots of different breeds of dogs, all with different characteristics, but they don't know what type of dog will suit them. Fortunately they have found some books in their local library that have the answers to lots of their questions.

Question: *How much exercise will my new dog need?*

Answer: There isn't a 'right' amount of exercise for dogs. Some dogs need much more exercise than others; a long walk for a tiny toy poodle would be quite a short walk for a huge Irish wolfhound. Dogs that were bred to do lots of running, such as Afghan hounds that were bred to chase deer, can get restless and behave badly if you can't give them enough exercise. Greyhounds make excellent family pets though. Because they were bred to run very fast for a short time, they are happier chasing a football round the garden for half an hour than going for a long walk.

Question: *Dog breeders talk about 'temperament'. What is it, and does it matter?*

Answer: Temperament is about how your dog behaves, and what mood he is in. Is he always friendly and pleased to see everyone, or does he get grumpy and want to be left alone? Does he play well with other dogs, or does he try to bite them? Terriers were bred to kill rats and rabbits, so they might snap at small animals – not a good idea if you have other pets. Some 'working dogs', such as sheep dogs, are very intelligent. They get bored easily and want you to play with them. They wouldn't be a good choice if you are out at work all day and want a quiet life when you get home!

poodle

Afghan hound

greyhound

Labrador

terrier

dachshund

spaniel

bulldog

sheep dog

Question: *How did bulldogs get such a strange shaped face, and is it true that they have breathing problems?*

Answer: Hundreds of years ago, bulldogs were bred for bull-baiting, where three or four dogs attacked a bull and killed it. Their strong, curved lower jaw meant they could hang on tightly, even when the bull tried to shake them off. Breeders chose the dogs that had the strongest, most curved lower jaws and bred from them. Then they chose the puppies with the strongest, most curved jaws and bred from them too, and so on, until all bulldogs had the shape of jaw you see today. As the bottom jaw got bigger, the top jaw got 'squashed'. This does make it harder for the dog to breathe, so bulldogs soon get out of breath if you make them run around too much.

Some other breeds have problems too. Dachshunds have very short legs and long backs; they often get back problems. Labradors are strong, but they are very heavy for their size and often get hip problems. Spaniels have very long ears that often get dirt in them and get infected.

Qs

- Imagine Harpreet and her family don't have much time to exercise a dog. Name one breed they shouldn't buy.

- Why might a terrier be a bad idea if you have other small pets?

- Explain why bulldogs get out of breath if they run around too much.

- List three other breeds of dogs that have health problems. Next to each breed, write what health problem it has.

Activities

- Imagine your family is going to buy a dog. Discuss what characteristics you would like, and why these characteristics are important for your family.

- Choose one breed of dog, perhaps your favourite breed. Use the internet to find some pictures and make a scrapbook about your breed. Include some information to tell people what your breed is like.

Designer babies

We inherit lots of characteristics from our parents, such as hair colour and eye colour. The information for them is stored in our genes, in the nucleus of each cell. Doctors can now test embryos to see which genes they have inherited, and have even altered some of the genes in animals. Reese and Benson have been finding out more about this.

Setting the scene

What do people think about embryo selection?

Embryo selection is a way of allowing parents to choose not to have a baby that would be seriously ill or handicapped. Some people think this is a great idea; others are not so happy about it.

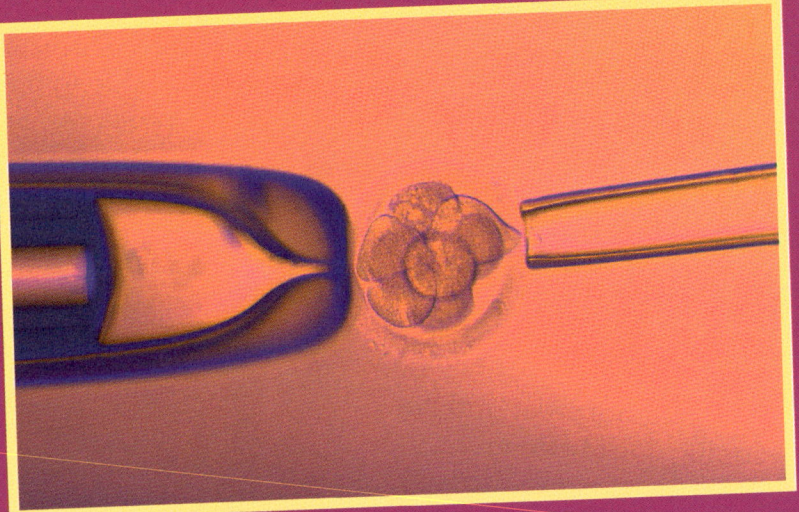

This is what parents-to-be Jake and Sue told Reese: 'We have a history of the genetic lung disease, cystic fibrosis, in both our families. People with cystic fibrosis can have difficulty breathing. They have to have uncomfortable treatment every day, and they may well die young from lung infections. We just didn't want to see our child suffer like that. Embryo selection is great. Doctors can look at our embryos while they are still only a few cells, and check they don't have the disease.'

Benson interviewed Mo from the Day Centre for disabled people. She isn't happy about embryo selection at all. 'It's completely wrong to interfere with nature. Some people seem to think disabled people are less important than "normal" people now. That's going to get a lot worse if parents can start throwing out babies that aren't perfect.'

BABY JAMES IS A LIFESAVER!

BABY JAMES, born last month, really is a very special baby. He was specially selected as an embryo, long before he was born, so that he is an exact tissue match for his older brother. His brother has a life-threatening illness that means he has to have a blood transfusion every three weeks. When baby James was born, doctors took special cells called stem cells from his umbilical cord. Doctors hope to transplant these cells into his older brother, where they will grow into the healthy blood cells he needs to completely cure him. Our reporter couldn't speak to the doctor or his parents, but a nurse told us 'When baby James is older, I hope his mum and dad will tell him how he was specially chosen to help his big brother.'

Who can decide what a 'perfect' person should look like? Do you think such a thing exists?

Human genetic engineering

There is a lot of confusion about what human genetic engineering can do. At present doctors can do embryo selection, which is testing embryos and rejecting the ones with genetic illnesses. One day it may be possible for scientists to create 'super humans' who are good-looking, clever, always healthy, and so on, but most scientists think that is a very long way off, if it ever happens at all. At the moment scientists don't even know what genes control most characteristics, and some genes are known to control lots of characteristics.

Doctors have done experiments on mice and some farm animals where they have replaced damaged genes in embryos with healthy genes. These new genes can be passed on to the animal's offspring. There are no plans to try this with humans, as it is only successful about 5% of the time. Also the new genes can cause changes in other characteristics, and scientists think that wouldn't be acceptable in humans.

I think all the work scientists are doing with human genes is great. You only have to listen to Jake and Sue to see how good it is.

That's only one side of the story. They only told you the good bits, so did the newspaper. The science magazine said a bit more about the experiments that scientists might be able to do soon. But it didn't really help me make up my mind about whether these experiments are a good idea or not.

Qs

- Explain in your own words what you think 'embryo selection' is.

- What will doctors do with the 'stem cells' from baby James?

- Why does Mo think embryo selection is a bad thing?

- Explain in your own words why scientists haven't tried replacing damaged genes with healthy genes in human embryos.

Activities

- Discuss your opinions about the scientific work mentioned in this article. Is it a good thing or a bad thing? Should it be allowed at all? Is it right in some circumstances and wrong in others? Who should decide whether or not it takes place?

- Write some questions for a questionnaire that you could use to find out what people think about human genetic engineering. (Most people are more likely to fill in questionnaires if the answers are just tick boxes.)

A clone of my own

When you think of cloning, do you think of hundreds of copies of you, all identical to each other? For some people the possibility of cloning humans is a wonderful scientific breakthrough, and an exciting opportunity. Other people see it as a real-life horror film. So what is cloning, and why do people feel so strongly, and so differently, about it? Read what our panel of experts has to say.

Setting the scene

Question: *What is cloning?*

Answer: When they talk about cloning in the newspapers and on TV they usually mean 'reproductive cloning'. This means making a whole new individual using the DNA from just one existing adult individual. DNA is the special material inside the nucleus of a cell that contains all the genetic information for the individual. When scientists talk about cloning, they might mean reproductive cloning, DNA cloning or therapeutic cloning. DNA cloning is where scientists put some of the DNA from an organism into bacteria to reproduce large amounts of the same DNA for research. Therapeutic cloning is also called 'embryo cloning' and it is the production of human stem cells for medical research.

Question: *When was Dolly the sheep cloned, and is she the only animal that has been cloned?*

Answer: Dolly the sheep was born in 1996. Scientists had cloned several animals before, including tadpoles, fish, mice, rabbits and pigs. Dolly was special because she was the first animal to be cloned from adult DNA, instead of from embryo cells. The DNA from cells from an adult sheep's udder was put into an egg cell whose nucleus had been removed. Chemicals were used to make the egg start dividing, then the embryo was put into an adult sheep, where it developed normally.

Scientists have since cloned hundreds of other animals like this, but less than 1% of all attempts are successful. They hope one day to be able to clone animals from endangered species like this, but at present there are lots of problems. Many of the cloned animals have poor health and die young from infections and other diseases. Dolly was put down in 2003, aged 6, suffering from lung cancer and arthritis, even though most sheep live to 11 or 12 years old.

Dolly the sheep

Question: *Have any humans ever been cloned?*

Answer: Some doctors claim that they have cloned humans. They have not allowed other doctors to see all their results, so most scientists don't believe them.

We're a long way from cloning like this. How would you feel if it became possible?

Question: *What medical research is therapeutic cloning used for?*

Answer: Therapeutic cloning is used to produce human stem cells. When an egg cell first starts dividing, all the cells are non-specialised stem cells that can grow into any kind of specialised cell. Medical researchers hope that one day these stem cells can be used to replace damaged cells in humans with heart disease, Alzheimer's disease, cancer and other diseases. They also hope that the stem cells can be grown into tissues and organs for transplants, with DNA exactly matching the DNA of the person needing the transplant. Many people object to therapeutic cloning because the stem cells are extracted from human embryos after they have divided for five days. The extraction process destroys the human embryo. This raises ethical concerns about when a human embryo becomes a potential person, and whether or not it is acceptable to produce human embryos to supply cells to cure diseases in other people.

Qs

- Explain what 'reproductive cloning' is.

- Describe how Dolly the sheep was cloned.

- Suggest a reason why stem cells are much more useful to medical researchers than cells from blood or tissue samples.

- Choose either 'therapeutic cloning' or 'reproductive cloning'. Make a two-column table to summarise some of the reasons for and against these types of cloning.

Activities

- Discuss what you think about cloning animals. Should it be done? If so, when and for what reason? Should there be any controls?

- Hold a 'conference style' discussion on therapeutic cloning. Different people in your group should take on the roles of different people who might be affected by it, such as medical researchers, people suffering from some of the illnesses that therapeutic cloning might cure, campaigners for the rights of the unborn child, and potential donors of the human eggs needed.

'Ban smoking' – which side are you on?

Setting the scene

You have learned that smoking damages the lungs, and smokers are more likely to suffer from other diseases as well. But nearly one-third of all adults in the UK smokes anyway, even though they know the risks. So what do teenagers think about smoking? This teenage magazine talks about some of the topics that have been in the news recently.

What do teenagers really think of smoking?

We went to the Bullring shopping centre in Birmingham to ask teenagers what they thought about smoking. We found there were lots of different views.

'I like smoking, it makes me feel grown up,' Kelly told us, 'I've never really thought about what might happen when I'm old.'

Jason said, 'I didn't really want to smoke, but all my friends do, and I didn't want them to think I was scared to.'

Mandy was very sure of what she felt about it. 'Some kids in my class smoke and it makes them stink. I don't like sitting next to them.'

Ireland bans smoking

In March 2004, Ireland became the first country in Europe to ban smoking in all workplaces. In 2002 and 2003, many cities around the world banned smoking in public places, the workplace, in restaurants or where there are children. In September 2004, five pub companies, with over 22 000 pubs in the UK, announced that their bars would be smoke-free by the end of 2004. Many smokers are not happy about the bans. But doctors and anti-smoking groups say it will cut the number of people who die from passive smoking, which is when people breathe in smoke from other people's cigarettes.

Union wants employers to pay for health insurance

Imagine you get a job working behind the bar in a smoky pub. Even though you don't smoke, you are always breathing in cigarette smoke from other people's cigarettes. Then in twenty years' time you get a disease caused by smoking. How would you feel if you had to pay for your own medical treatment? A union representing people who work in pubs is worried that this might happen to some of their members. They want the owners of the pubs to pay for health insurance for their workers, to pay the cost of any medical bills they might get.

Nicotine vaccine?

In 2002, a medical company in Florida started testing a vaccine that would stop people getting addicted to nicotine from cigarettes. Some people have suggested that, if the tests work, this vaccine should be given to teenagers. But people are asking lots of questions, such as 'Should all teenagers be given the vaccine, whether they want it or not?' and 'Should a teenager decide whether or not to have the vaccine, or should their parents or doctor choose for them?' Nobody has the answers to these questions yet.

Tobacco companies should pay compensation

Nowadays everyone knows smoking is bad for you. Cigarette packets have large warnings on them saying things such as 'Smoking kills'. But years ago people even thought smoking was good for you! Some people, who started smoking before people knew how dangerous it was, say the tobacco companies should pay them money to make up for the diseases the cigarettes have caused. But most tobacco companies say the people don't deserve any money because they should have given up smoking long ago.

Qs

- When did some cities around the world ban smoking in public places?

- What is passive smoking?

- Write down one of the questions people are asking about a nicotine vaccine.

- Explain what the union representing people who work in pubs is worried about.

Activities

- In November 2004, the government announced a four-year plan to make nearly all enclosed public areas smoke-free. Discuss whether you agree or disagree with this. Why?

- Imagine a teenage smoker, his or her Mum, and his or her doctor are talking about the new nicotine vaccine. Role-play the conversation they might have. Try to imagine what each of them would think.

Illegal drugs – prescribe them or not?

Recreational drugs are harmful, whether they are illegal drugs or legal ones such as alcohol, tobacco or caffeine. But a number of people have reported that illegal drugs actually improve certain illnesses. These articles from an imaginary medical journal show how doctors try to evaluate these reports, and decide whether or not certain illegal drugs should be prescribed for some patients.

Ecstasy may help post-traumatic stress disorder patients

N-methyl-3,4-methylenedioxyphenylisopropylamine (more commonly called Ecstasy or MDMA) is a mind-altering drug that was developed by a German company before the First World War. Scientists then forgot about it until its rediscovery in the 1960s. The drug was banned in the 1980s because it was dangerous – just a single Ecstasy tablet can kill. But even before it was banned, doctors were claiming that the drug was useful in helping people who had suffered serious trauma. People like soldiers who had seen friends killed or women who had been raped were able to relax enough to benefit from therapy when given the drug. Now new trials of the drug are being carried out to see if Ecstasy really does have any medical benefits. An American doctor commented 'It's really important that people understand that using the drug in these carefully controlled trials is nothing like kids using the drug illegally, which can be extremely dangerous.'

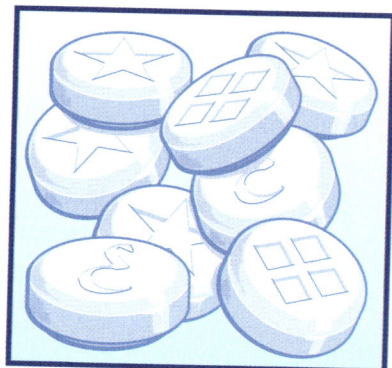

Ecstasy is one of the more dangerous illegal drugs, but doctors believe it may have some medical uses.

Can Ecstasy improve Parkinson's disease?

Tim Lawrence used to be a stuntman, using his brilliant physical skills to carry out all sorts of daring stunts for films. Then he got Parkinson's disease, a disease that usually only affects elderly people. Now, most of the time, his muscles either twitch uncontrollably, or 'freeze up' so he can't move at all. But Tim claims that when he takes Ecstasy illegally he gets control of his muscles again. 'It's like I don't have the disease at all – I can even do backflips and somersaults' he says. Doctors know that there are very serious health risks from taking Ecstasy; it affects chemicals in the brain and causes long-term damage to a person's memory and their ability to learn. But doctors also know they cannot ignore the benefits to people like Tim. The challenge is to find a new drug that has the benefits of Ecstasy without the long-term health risk.

Cannabis trials for multiple sclerosis patients

A British study into the use of cannabis to treat multiple sclerosis, a disease where nerve damage causes loss of muscle control, pain and disability, showed mixed results. Of the 630 patients who took part in the study, after 15 weeks most patients reported that the cannabis helped their pain and muscle stiffness. It helped them to walk more easily but it didn't improve their tiredness. However, doctors assessed how well their patients could move and walk before and after taking the drug, and they said there was no difference. The doctor carrying out the study said this difference in results might be because the cannabis affects how patients feel pain and discomfort. When some patients continued to take the cannabis for a further 12 months, doctors saw a marked improvement in their muscle stiffness and mobility. The Multiple Sclerosis Society is calling for cannabis to be made legal for multiple sclerosis sufferers. 'We believe lots of people could benefit' they said. Some doctors fear that if the drug stays illegal, multiple sclerosis patients will smoke it illegally anyway to relieve their symptoms, which will greatly increase their risk of getting lung cancer.

Doctors and patients do not completely agree about whether cannabis helps multiple sclerosis sufferers.

Qs

- How did doctors claim that Ecstasy could help trauma victims?

- How does Parkinson's disease affect Tim Lawrence? How does he say that Ecstasy helps him?

- After the 15-week study, patients and doctors said different things about how taking cannabis affects multiple sclerosis sufferers. What did they say?

- How did the doctor carrying out the study into the effects of cannabis explain this difference?

Activities

- Imagine you were like Tim Lawrence, and you knew that a drug would have short-term benefits, but would cause you long-term harm. Discuss how you would decide whether or not you wanted to take the drug.

- The Multiple Sclerosis Society wants cannabis to be available for multiple sclerosis sufferers. Role-play a discussion between members of the Society and the police, who are worried that the drug might get into the hands of people who would sell it or use it illegally.

Alternative medicine – truth or con?

Setting the scene

O ver many years, modern Western medicine has developed drugs and surgical techniques that are more and more specific in their effects, gradually curing or controlling more and more illnesses that used to be untreatable. Most of us are now so used to Western medicine 'curing everything' that we have forgotten that any other types of medicine exist. Our doctor explains what alternative medicines are, and what they have to offer in the treatment of disease.

Many alternative medicines, such as aromatherapy, concentrate on treating the whole person to make a patient feel more relaxed and comfortable.

Interviewer Tell us, doctor, what are alternative medicines?

Doctor They are anything people use to treat themselves instead of going to their doctor. Alternative medicines include herbal medicines, folk medicines and faith healing. People use treatments like acupuncture to relieve pain or instead of anaesthetics at the same time as modern Western medicine. Doctors call these treatments 'complementary medicine'.

Interviewer You're going too fast for me. Could you explain what some of those things you mentioned are, please?

Doctor Well, herbal medicines are medicines made from plants. People have been using herbal medicines for thousands of years. Folk medicines are what you might call 'old fashioned' remedies. Some of them, such as leeches, are turning out to be really good, others, such as swallowing a fried mouse to cure a sore throat, probably don't do any good at all! Faith healing is using the power of prayer to cure illnesses.

Interviewer So if I decided I wanted to use alternative medicines, who would I go to?

Doctor That's part of the problem. Doctors fear that many 'alternative medicine doctors' know nothing at all about diseases or the human body, and some are certainly doing a lot of harm. Deciding who is good and who isn't is difficult.

Interviewer What harm can they do? Surely these treatments aren't actually harmful?

Doctor Some folk medicines and herbal medicines contain powerful chemical ingredients. If they are given for the wrong illness or in the wrong amount they can cause serious illness. Many diseases are easier to cure if they are detected early, so even harmless treatments can cause problems if they mean a person doesn't go to see their doctor until they've had a disease for a long time. Also some herbal medicines may stop 'ordinary'

medicines working properly. For example, taking St John's wort, a mild herbal anti-depressant, makes the contraceptive pill less effective. In Sweden, manufacturers have to explain this on packets of St John's wort, but they don't have to in the UK.

Interviewer You sound as if you disapprove of all forms of alternative medicine.

Doctor I'm afraid doctors do often give that impression. I didn't mean to. It's just that we doctors are used to giving people treatments that have been scientifically tested and shown to work. I wouldn't mind using alternative medicine treatments that I knew would work.

Interviewer Are there any?

Doctor Oh yes, we keep finding 'alternative medicines' that are so good we start using them. But we need more proper scientific testing to tell the good from the bad.

Interviewer Tell us about some of the things that work.

Doctor Well, acupuncture is so good it is often used as a 'complementary' medicine to help patients cope with severe pain. We aren't quite sure why it works. We think it is something to do with stimulating the body's own electrical signals, but clinical trials have shown it does work. New antibiotics are being found in plant remedies that have been used for hundreds of years; leeches have been shown to help healing in severe burns or badly infected wounds; and surveys have shown that people with a religious faith are generally healthier than those without; we don't know why.

Interviewer Well, thank you doctor. You've certainly given me food for thought.

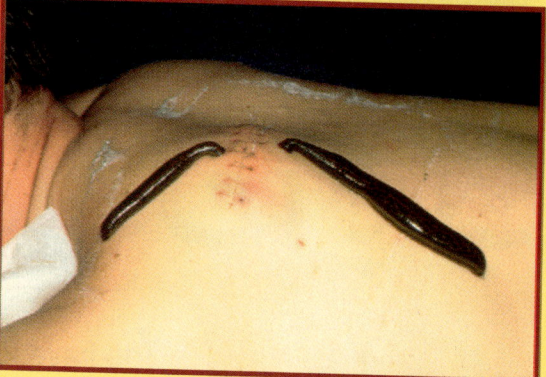

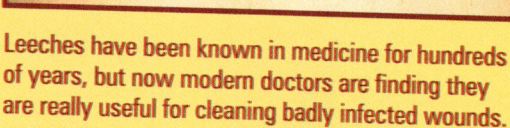
Leeches have been known in medicine for hundreds of years, but now modern doctors are finding they are really useful for cleaning badly infected wounds.

Qs

- What is the difference between alternative medicine and complementary medicine?

- Describe one reason why many doctors are opposed to alternative medicines.

- Many of the conventional medicines that we use were originally developed from plant ingredients. Suggest some reasons why most doctors feel these medicines are safer than herbal medicines.

Activities

- Discuss how you feel about alternative medicines. Would you be happy to use any of them? What advantages do you think they might have? Is there any scientific research you would like to see done to find out more about them?

- Suppose some parents with a seriously ill child wanted to use alternative medicines instead of conventional medicines on their child. Is it acceptable for them to do so? Who should have the right to make such decisions about medical treatment for a child?

Too much of a good thing!

Getting the scene

You have learned that green plants use their leaves for photosynthesis, to make their own food from sunlight. The plants need good roots and good soil, so they can get the water and minerals they need to grow healthy leaves. *The Garden Gang* is a new television programme where a group of teenagers put what they know about plants to the test, as they try to design and grow the best garden. Our expert James tells us how they are getting on.

Programme One – Getting your hands dirty

Well, I'm pleased to see our Garden Gang has got the right attitude. You don't get anywhere with a garden until you get your hands dirty! They have used sticks and string to mark out where they want the flowerbeds and the pond and now they're digging. Digging is really, really good for a garden; it breaks up hard soil into fine bits with spaces between them. That means more air and more water can get into the soil for plant roots. They're mixing in animal manure too. That's even better. The well-rotted manure they've chosen isn't smelly, and it contains lots of nitrogen. Plants need nitrogen, and the extra nitrogen from the manure will really give these plants a head start.

Programme Two – It's growing well

We've got a lot to show you since you last visited the garden. The pond is full of water and some of the water plants are even flowering. The flower borders are looking really good – I just love the colour scheme. It was worth the hard work digging and mixing in all that manure. To keep the plants growing strongly all summer, the Garden Gang has been adding 'slow release' nitrogen fertiliser pellets to the border, to keep a good supply of nitrogen in the soil. I just hope they're not overdoing it – too much nitrogen is actually bad for the plants. I'm a bit worried they've just been chucking the pellets around without reading the instructions carefully.

Programme Three – The pond stinks!

As you can see, we're having a bit of a problem with the pond – you're lucky you can't smell it! The water has gone black and smelly and the plants are dying off, except for a thick mat of slimy green algae across the top few centimetres. The problem is all those nitrogen pellets the Garden Gang was using. Some of the nitrogen has washed out of the flower borders into the pond. It has made the algae grow really well, so well that the plants underneath can't get any sunlight and they're dying. And because the plants in the water make oxygen, there's not much oxygen at the bottom of the pond either. If we had fish in here, they'd all be floating on their backs on the surface!

Programme Four – Everything in the garden's lovely!

The Garden Gang has fixed the smelly pond problem, and the garden's looking great again. 'We thought the best thing to do was to pull out all the green algae, so sunlight could get to the bottom of the pond again,' Anila told us, 'so we just put on our wellies, rolled up our sleeves and got stuck in.' And you can see it has worked! Getting more sunlight has helped the plants to grow, they have given off oxygen and this has made the water clear and fresh again. Rivers and lakes sometimes have this problem too because of nitrogen fertiliser from fields, but unfortunately there is no one there to pull out the algae.

Qs

- Suggest some things plants need to grow healthy leaves.

- What does the animal manure put into the soil have that is good for plants?

- Why is it important to read the instructions on how to use the nitrogen fertiliser?

- What happened to the pond when it got too much nitrogen in it?

- Describe how pulling the algae out of the pond made the water clear and fresh again.

Activities

- Imagine the pond next to your school playing field is black and smelly. You think it might be because fertiliser is running into it from the nearby fields. Discuss what you can do about it. Should you try to fix it yourself, complain to the farmer, or do something else?

- Jack says 'If a little bit of fertiliser is good for my vegetable plants, then lots will be even better.' Make a leaflet or poster to explain to him why it's important to use the right amount of fertiliser.

What are GM foods?

Setting the scene

You may well have heard of GM foods or GM crops. Scientists have been carrying out trials to grow GM crops, politicians have been deciding if farmers should be allowed to grow them, and supermarkets have been deciding whether or not to sell GM foods. So what are they, and why do lots of people feel so strongly about them? Read this interview with Owen, a farmer involved in the trials of GM crops.

Interviewer Good morning, Owen. Tell us about the GM crops you've been growing but, since I don't even know what GM crops are, can you tell us that first please?

Owen GM stands for 'genetically modified'. GM crops are plants where scientists have used genetic engineering to change the genes in the plant, to alter some of its characteristics. GM foods are foods that have been made from GM crops.

Interviewer What's the point of genetically modifying plants?

Owen It's a way of improving the plants so harvests are better.

Interviewer So how does that work?

Owen For thousands of years, farmers have improved their crops by selecting, and breeding from, the best plants. But it takes many, many years to improve plants in this way. When scientists genetically modify plants, they can make the changes happen immediately.

Interviewer I think I see. So what sort of changes are we talking about?

Owen Some of the changes made so far include making plants more drought-resistant, so they grow better in dry soils; making plants more disease-resistant, so they aren't damaged so much by pests; and making plants that can be digested more easily, so they are more nutritious and animals don't need to eat so much of them.

Interviewer All those changes sound really good, so why do some people say GM crops are such a bad thing?

Owen People have all sorts of worries about GM crops. Sometimes they worry that they might be poisonous, or less nutritious than non-GM crops. Lots of people are concerned about how they might affect the environment. If GM crops that have been made inedible for insect pests cross with wild plants, they might make them inedible too. Then there might be fewer insects, which means less food for birds and small mammals. Some species may even go extinct.

Interviewer So is it sensible to grow them at all?

Owen That's what the trials are to find out. They will tell us things like how likely it is that GM crops will affect other plants nearby, and whether they really can be grown using less fertiliser or weedkiller than for normal crops. Some people say GM crops are actually good for the environment, because farmers have to use much less pesticides on them, which leaves more wildlife in the fields.

Interviewer And what do you think?

Owen I think we have to find out more about them. And we should remember that they are all different; some may be harmless, others may not be. We have to look at the risks and the advantages of each type of GM crop.

Interviewer So who should decide if GM crops are grown or not?

Owen Ah. That's a very difficult question. I don't know the answer. I think governments will probably have to decide, but I think they should listen carefully to the scientists and also to all the other people who have concerns about GM crops. It's difficult asking the general public to decide because often they don't really know enough about it – I didn't know anything about GM crops myself until I took part in these trials.

Interviewer Well, thank you for talking to us, Owen.

Qs

○ What are GM crops?

○ Describe two ways in which plants have been genetically modified.

○ How do people fear GM crops may affect the environment?

○ What do you think the trials of GM crops are trying to find out?

Activities

■ People in developing countries are usually in favour of GM crops, because farmers who grow GM crops can grow more food more cheaply than they can with non-GM crops. Discuss whether you think developing countries should be allowed to grow GM crops, and if the possible effects on the environment matter?

■ Discuss who you think should make the decisions about growing GM crops. Should it be politicians, scientists, individual farmers, or members of the public? Why do you think it should be these people?

Talking to plants – are you mad?

You have learned how plants use photosynthesis to make their own food from sunlight. You have probably learned the roles that healthy leaves, healthy roots, the correct temperatures and the correct mixture of nutrients in the soil all play in making plants grow well. But have you ever heard gardeners claim that talking to their plants makes them grow? This gardener wonders if these claims can possibly be right.

Setting the scene

7TH APRIL

All the seeds I planted in my greenhouse are coming up well. My neighbour is quite jealous. He says his plants never seem to grow as well as mine do. I told him it's because I talk to my plants. He said that's a load of nonsense, but I can't help wondering. I've always talked to my plants and they've always grown well. There must be something in it.

10TH APRIL

I've got really fascinated by this talking to plants business. I was discussing it with Jim the other day and he says it's rubbish too. He says my plants grow well because during the time I spend with them when I talk to them, I notice all sorts of other things like whether or not they need weeding, or watering or re-potting. I suppose he might be right. I feel quite sad, I like talking to my plants!

11TH APRIL

Talking to plants does work! The man at the garden centre said he read it in a book once. A scientist was saying how when you talk to plants you are breathing out all over them, and your breath contains lots more carbon dioxide than ordinary air. Plants need carbon dioxide for photosynthesis: the extra carbon dioxide helps them photosynthesise faster, so they make more energy and grow faster. So it looks like it doesn't matter whether you talk to them or just spend a lot of time looking at them and breathing out all over them.

13TH APRIL

The more I find out about carbon dioxide and plants the worse it gets! I was reading about plant growth and global warming in a science magazine in the library the other day. It said that plants grow better if they have more carbon dioxide, but global warming is making the climate warmer and wetter and that makes plants grow slower. So now I don't know whether breathing out over my plants will make them grow better because they get more carbon dioxide or worse because my breath is warm and wet!

15TH APRIL

I've been reading that science magazine at the library again, and I've decided that it's probably alright to breathe out all over my flowers but I probably shouldn't breathe over my vegetables! Another article said scientists are worried that global warming is making food less nutritious. Apparently they have found that the extra carbon dioxide that causes global warming makes food plants grow more quickly, but then they don't absorb so many minerals from the soil. So I suppose that if I breathe out all over my vegetables, the extra carbon dioxide will make them grow quickly but they won't be so good for me when I eat them. It's all so confusing. I think I'm just going to talk to all my plants as usual and enjoy it!

Qs

- On 10th April, what reasons did the neighbour suggest for why the gardener's plants are growing well?

- Explain in your own words why extra carbon dioxide increases the growth rate of plants.

- The gardener fears that his warm, wet breath will make his plants grow more slowly. Why does he think this, and do you agree with him? Give a reason for your answer.

- Draw a two-column table listing the positive and negative effects of global warming and extra carbon dioxide on plant growth.

Activities

- Role-play a discussion between several gardeners at a gardening club who are trying to decide whether or not talking to their plants is going to have any effect on the way the plants grow.

- Use the internet to research the latest ideas about how carbon dioxide might affect plant growth.

Witchcraft

Lots of our food comes directly from plants. Imagine walking round a supermarket buying breakfast cereal, cakes, coffee, tea, bread and orange juice. All these, and many more, are made from plants. We are lucky to eat plants from all over the world, but it has not always been like that. People used to eat a much smaller range of different foods. Read this detective story to find out a problem this caused and also how scientists solved a puzzle that was hundreds of years old.

The puzzle

You probably know that hundreds of years ago people believed in witches. They used to burn them at the stake and drown them in duck ponds. But historical records show this didn't happen very often. Witch hunts would usually start about harvest time, and last for a few months. Then they would stop and there might not be any more for years and years. So modern historians and scientists began to wonder why. Perhaps the witches weren't witches at all, perhaps they were ill.

Finding the clues

There are lots of stories about the witch hunts. Modern scientists read these to find their clues. Some stories are all about how the witches behaved. Scientists compared these stories with modern medical records to see if they could find out whether the witches had an illness. Other accounts list the places where witch hunts happened. Had all these places got anything in common with each other? The last clue was to do with prices and weather. There were more witches after a cold winter and a wet spring! The bad weather made some crops grow badly, so the harvest was poor and the prices went up.

Putting the clues together

Most of the witch stories say that the witches were 'dancing about' or twitching. Many of them talk about the witches seeing things that weren't there. Some poisons affect people like this, so these stories made scientists think perhaps the witches were being poisoned by something. All the witch hunts happened in places where the people ate bread made from rye grain. In areas where the bread was made from other cereals, there were no witch hunts. So it looked like the witches might be being poisoned by rye. But how? Cold winters and wet springs make a fungus called ergot grow on rye. And the symptoms of ergot poisoning are just like the symptoms the witches seemed to have. Problem solved!

Ergot today?

So why don't we get lots of people with ergot poisoning today after a cold winter and then a wet spring? There are lots of reasons. Today we are much wealthier. If our cereal crop grows with black mould on it, we can throw it away; we won't starve if we don't eat it. Farmers have fungicide sprays they can use if they see ergot starting to grow on their rye crop. Also most of us eat bread made from wheat, not from rye. Ergot poisoning does still happen. Ergot is used to make the illegal drug called LSD. The 'high' people get when they use LSD is actually poisoning – which is why many people die after taking it.

Qs

○ List five different foods that are made from plants.

○ When did witch hunts happen? How long did they last?

○ Where did scientists look for clues about witch hunts?

○ Describe one of the clues they found. What did it tell scientists?

○ Give one reason why ergot poisoning is uncommon today.

Activities

■ Imagine you have just discovered one of the clues about witches and witch hunts. Role-play the telephone call you make to a friend to tell them all about it.

■ Use the internet to find out some more about witches. You could begin your search using the words 'Salem' and 'witches'.

Yes, we have no bananas

Do you like bananas? They are a very popular fruit in Britain. Many supermarkets have more bananas for sale than any other fruit. Yet scientists fear that the sweet, yellow banana we are all so used to may be extinct in 10 years' time. What could possibly be going wrong? Our expert explains.

Why don't bananas have pips?

Most of the fruit we eat has pips, like apples or strawberries, or stones, like peaches, plums and cherries. You already know that these pips or stones are the seeds that grow into new plants or trees, which grow more fruit. But have you ever wondered why bananas don't have pips or stones? It's because the bananas we eat are sterile; they do not grow seeds, and they cannot reproduce to produce new plants. Banana growers get new plants by taking cuttings (pieces of stem) from the old plants and growing the cuttings into new plants. This means that all the cultivated, sweet bananas around the world are almost identical to each other. That can be good, because growers know all the new banana plants will produce fruit just as good as the old plants did. But it can be very bad, because a disease that kills one plant is quite likely to kill all the plants.

So where are banana growers slipping up?

Banana growers are finding that more and more of their banana plants are being killed by fungus that grows on the banana plants. The growers spray their banana plants with fungicides, chemicals that kill the fungus, but gradually the fungus is becoming immune to the chemicals and the fungicides are becoming less and less effective. They fear that one type of fungus, the Sigotoka fungus, is spreading so fast that it will kill all cultivated, sweet bananas in the next 10 years. Normally if this happens to a crop, growers cross their plants with another variety of the same plant that is immune to the fungus, but banana growers can't do that, because sweet bananas are sterile, and don't cross with other plants. A few cultivated bananas are not sterile, and could be crossed with wild bananas that are resistant to the Sigotoka fungus, but the wild bananas are full of seeds and inedible.

Will bananas really go extinct?

We don't know yet. Although we think of bananas as a sweet, yellow fruit, there are actually lots of different types of bananas around the world. Over 400 million people in developing countries near the equator rely on bananas as their staple food. They eat varieties of bananas called plantains or matooke bananas, which look like large green bananas. These bananas are boiled, steamed, fried or roasted, and in East Africa they are even made into a nutritious low-alcohol beer. Scientists have used genetic engineering to cure a disease in matooke bananas, by adding a gene from rice to the matooke banana plants. They hope they might be able to put a gene from wild bananas into sweet bananas to make them resistant to the Sigotoka fungus, without losing the flavour and texture that people like so much. We will just have to wait and see.

Qs

- How do banana growers get new banana plants?

- Give one advantage and one disadvantage of all cultivated, sweet banana plants being almost identical.

- What do you think might happen to cultivated bananas if they were crossed successfully with wild bananas?

- Explain in your own words how scientists hope to prevent sweet, cultivated bananas from becoming extinct.

Activities

- If sweet, cultivated bananas did go extinct, discuss all the people who might be affected, and how it would affect them.

- Find out some more about cooking bananas (plantain or matooke). Can you find out any recipes that use them? Make a recipe card, poster or leaflet to show how they are eaten.

Farming, the organic way

Getting the scene

Almost all supermarkets now sell organic food; perhaps you buy it. But how much do most of us actually know about it? You've probably heard people saying 'It's good for you,' 'It's very expensive,' 'It's got less chemicals in it,' 'It tastes great,' 'It tastes exactly the same,' and lots of other things. But how different is organic food and do organic farmers really do anything different from other farmers?

What is organic farming?

Modern farming methods generally use a large variety of different chemicals for fertilising the soil, and killing weeds and pests. Organic farming is growing food crops without using these chemicals. Many people think this means that the farmers just plant the seed and wait for it to grow, but that is not so. Organic farmers still have to keep the soil fertile and stop their crops being destroyed by pests or choked by weeds, but to do this they use a range of different methods that avoid the use of chemicals which have a large effect on the environment.

Getting rid of pests and weeds

Food crops are attacked by a wide range of insect pests that multiply rapidly because there is a good supply of food. Most farming uses chemical insecticides to kill these insects. Organic farming relies on the larvae of other insects, called beneficial insects, to eat the eggs of insect pests. To encourage the large number of beneficial insects that are needed, organic farmers plant the borders of their fields with 'host crops', crops that provide shelter and food for adult insects. The levels of beneficial insects on organic farms are much higher than on most farms, since the insecticides used on most farms to kill pest insects also kill the beneficial insects.

All these insects are beneficial insects; their larvae eat the eggs of pest species of insect.

Weeds can be an expensive problem on organic farms, since weeding is done by hand or by tractor. Organic farmers try to limit the number of weeds growing in their fields by watering the fields to encourage weed seeds to germinate before crops are planted. The young weed plants are then ploughed in before the crop is sown. Farmers also plant 'cover crops', crops that form such a dense layer that weeds cannot grow. These 'cover crops' are then ploughed in. These measures lead to a gradual reduction in the number of weeds on organic farms, over a few years.

How do organic farmers keep the soil fertile?

Organic farmers do use fertilisers, but they are organic fertilisers, such as ploughed in 'cover crops', and industrial waste like liquid fish slurry or used mushroom compost, which is heated before use to kill bacteria and weed seeds. Increasing the amount of dead plant and animal material in the soil also has the benefit of making the soil hold water better, so crops need less watering in dry weather.

What do organic farmers do if their crop gets diseased?

All crops are affected occasionally by bacteria or fungi that cause disease. Conventional farming uses chemical fungicides to kill these. Organic farmers have to rely on crop rotation, which is planting different crops in a field each year, so that populations of disease-causing bacteria or fungi do not build up. Organically grown plants are generally healthier and more immune to disease than conventionally farmed plants, but occasionally organic farmers lose most or all of a crop to disease.

Qs

- List three ways in which farmers have to care for their crops and soil, to ensure a good harvest.

- Explain what is meant by 'beneficial insects'. How do organic farmers increase the number of beneficial insects in their fields?

- Many people claim that organic farming is 'good for the environment'. Suggest some ways in which they might be right, or wrong.

- Organic food is generally more expensive than non-organic food. Suggest some possible reasons why.

Activities

- Carry out a survey of people in your class to find out whether or not their families ever buy organic foods. Find out about their reasons for either buying it or not buying it.

- Some people claim that organic food is 'good for you' because it has 'less chemicals' in it. Do some research to find out what 'chemicals' people worry about in conventionally farmed food. Discuss whether or not you think they should worry.

Metal poisoning

You have learned that there are lots of different metals – you may even know properties of quite a few of them. You probably know that many of the chemical reactions using metals make useful new materials, but some reactions, such as iron going rusty, are a nuisance. These newspaper reports tell us how chemical reactions between metals and our bodies can be really dangerous.

Setting the scene

Justice for Bhopal – when will the people stop suffering?

THIRTY YEARS AGO, after an accident at a factory making pesticides, lots of mercury got into the soil and water round Bhopal in central India. 'People are still dying,' an aid worker told us. 'Mercury causes brain damage and kidney damage. Even the unborn children aren't safe – mercury harms them too.'

'The chemical company shut down the factory after the accident,' a man living in Bhopal explained. 'But they didn't clean up the mercury in the ponds around the town. They tell us not to drink the water, but we have nothing else to drink. We have to use the water to water our crops too. They made this mess. They are killing our children. They should clean it up.'

Editor's note: Have you heard the saying 'mad as a hatter'? Hat makers in the 19th century used mercury for hat making and it sent them mad.

ONE IN TEN BRITISH CHILDREN HAVE LEAD POISONING!

Health experts say that as many as one in ten children in the UK may have lead in their blood. 'Even small amounts of lead lower children's IQ,' one health expert told us. 'That makes it harder for them to concentrate, and can cause problems such as speech and behaviour problems, ADHD, hearing loss and clumsiness.'

We found out that most of the lead comes from the soil and from old lead paint. Lead used to be added to petrol to make car engines run better. Lead in petrol was banned in the UK at the end of 1999, but there is still a lot of lead dust in the soil, especially near main roads. Lead dust can also come from old or flaking paint. 'Babies and toddlers are most at risk, because they keep putting their hands in their mouths, but parents shouldn't panic,' health experts tell us, 'if you live in an old house, you should wipe up dust on windowsills and paintwork with a damp cloth. Wash children's hands before they eat, and after they have been playing outside. Feed children foods with plenty of iron and calcium to stop the lead being absorbed by the body.'

The biggest mass poisoning in history – whose fault is it?

In the 1970s, before many of our readers were born, we told you about children dying in Bangladesh from diseases caused by drinking dirty water. A quarter of a million children were dying each year. Then we told you how the problem had been solved. International aid organisations dug wells, so clean drinking water could be pumped up from deep underground. Local people called it 'devil's water' and now it seems they were right!

Doctors from Bangladesh are reporting villagers coming to them with blisters on their hands and feet and the early stages of cancer – both signs of arsenic poisoning. It turns out that the arsenic is in the rocks deep underground, and it is in the water being pumped to the wells at the surface. The people who dug the wells didn't test the water for arsenic. The World Health Organisation fears that half of the 10 million wells may be poisoned, and tens or even hundreds of thousands of people may die. It is probably the biggest poisoning case in history – but we're asking you 'Whose fault is it?'

Qs

- List two parts of the body that mercury damages.

- List some problems that lead causes.

- Who is most at risk from lead poisoning, and why?

- Where was the arsenic in the Bangladeshi water coming from?

- How many wells in Bangladesh may be affected, and how many people may die?

Activities

- Some people say it is the international aid organisations' fault that people are dying of arsenic poisoning in Bangladesh. Do you agree? Discuss whether digging the wells was right or wrong, and what should be done now.

- Make a poster for your local Health Centre, telling parents about the risks of lead poisoning and telling them what they can do about it.

Iron that won't rust

Setting the scene

You know that iron and steel (which is mostly made of iron) go rusty. They react with oxygen to form iron oxide, that we call rust. Yet there has been an ancient, unpainted, iron pillar in Delhi, in India, for 1600 years and it still isn't rusty! Scientists wanted to know why, and now Indian experts think they have cracked the problem.

The pillar at Delhi is very impressive. It stands at the centre of the oldest Moslem mosque in Delhi. Historians think it was erected in the fourth century AD, though some people say it is over 2000 years old. It is nearly 7 metres high, has a diameter of about 40 centimetres and is estimated to weigh about 6 tonnes. At about eye level, it is so highly polished that it is sometimes mistaken for bronze.

It's probably the weather!

At first, scientists thought it was the weather in Delhi that stopped the iron pillar rusting. You know that iron goes rusty more quickly if it is damp; indoors, where it is dry, biscuit tins or tea caddies don't go rusty at all. Delhi has about the same annual rainfall as London, but it is not spread evenly throughout the year; there are about 20 days a year when it is really wet, but nearly all the rest of the time it is dry. The scientists found this wasn't the reason the pillar isn't rusty though when they looked at modern iron in Delhi. The modern iron in Delhi goes rusty. Also iron objects of about the same age in other, much wetter, parts of India are also almost rust-free.

It must be the way it's made

Scientists' next guess was that the iron of the iron pillar in Delhi was somehow different from modern iron. So they got permission to take tiny samples of iron from the pillar and analyse them. They found that the iron contains about 1% phosphorus, compared with less than 0.05% phosphorus in modern iron. This is because the limestone used in modern blast furnaces to make iron removes almost all of the phosphorus and other impurities. The phosphorus in the iron pillar binds with iron, hydrogen and oxygen to make a very thin coating of a chemical called 'iron hydrogen phosphate hydrate' that protects the pillar from air and moisture, so it can't go rusty. The phosphate in the coating also explains why the pillar looks a bronze colour, instead of the more usual silvery colour of iron. Scientists now think the iron makers of ancient India added phosphorus deliberately to stop the iron going rusty, because even older iron from India does not have large amounts of phosphorus in it.

Can we learn from this?

Scientists are now investigating how the protective layer forms on iron with a large amount of phosphorus in it. They want to know if phosphorus could be added to modern steel to make a similar protective coating form on the steel. If it works, steel that won't rust for thousands of years would be very useful for building bridges, railways and buildings; it might even be possible to use it to make containers to store nuclear waste safely.

Qs

- Describe the rainfall in Delhi, compared with the rainfall in London.

- How did scientists find out what chemicals are in the iron that the iron pillar is made from?

- Why doesn't modern iron contain large amounts of phosphorus?

- Describe briefly in your own words how the phosphorus stops the pillar going rusty.

- What evidence makes scientists think the ancient Indian craftsmen added phosphorus deliberately?

Activities

- At the moment we usually stop steel going rusty by painting or varnishing it. Discuss as many reasons as you can why non-rusting steel might be better, what sort of things it would be really useful for and why.

- One of the ideas scientists had to explain why the iron pillar in Delhi didn't rust was 'It's the weather'. Make a list of the evidence that supports this idea and a second list of the evidence that doesn't support it.

Shipwrecked?

Have you heard of the *Mary Rose*? If you are really lucky you may even have seen it in Portsmouth. It is a wooden Tudor warship, from Henry VIII's navy, that sank in 1545. On 11th October 1982 an estimated 60 million television viewers worldwide watched as the *Mary Rose* was lifted to the surface. Our expert explains how scientists have worked since then to stop the *Mary Rose* rotting away or falling apart.

Setting the scene

Problem 1: Stop it falling apart

Water soaks into wood; we say the wood becomes waterlogged. A wooden ship such as the *Mary Rose* absorbs about 1.5 kg of sea water for every 1 kg of wood. We wanted to put the *Mary Rose* on display to the public, but we couldn't let it dry out because if we did the wood would simply fall apart. So we put the *Mary Rose* on display in a specially built museum, where the wreck was sprayed with chilled fresh water, 24 hours a day for 12 years. During this time we had to decide on a way to preserve the *Mary Rose* permanently.

Problem 2: Preserve the wood

Finding a way to preserve the wood was difficult. We had to find something that would soak into the wood and replace the water; otherwise when the water dried out of the wood, the wood would lose its shape and fall apart. We couldn't paint preservative on, because the pieces of wood are so thick that it would never soak in far enough. We solved the problem using a water-soluble wax called polyethylene glycol. In 1994, we began a 10-year programme to spray the *Mary Rose* with polyethylene glycol. Clear screens in front of the ship allow visitors to see the *Mary Rose* without them coming into contact with the preservative. When all the wood is soaked in the wax we can then begin a very slow drying-out process.

Problem 3: An unexpected problem

At first, spraying with polyethylene glycol seemed an ideal way to save ancient ships such as the *Mary Rose*. Then we found a problem no one had foreseen. When the *Mary Rose* was underwater, bacteria from the seabed started to feed on the wood, as part of a normal decay process. The bacteria got the oxygen they needed from sulphates in the sea water. This turned the sulphates into hydrogen sulphide, which was gradually absorbed into the wood. Now that the ship has been raised, the hydrogen sulphide in the wood is combining with oxygen from the air to make sulphuric acid, which is destroying the wood.

Normally this reaction would be quite slow and not a serious worry, but the polyethylene glycol wax we are using is making iron nails in the ship corrode. The corroded iron is spreading through the wood and acting as a catalyst to speed up the reaction between hydrogen sulphide and oxygen. We have to find a way to neutralise the sulphuric acid before ships such as the *Mary Rose* are destroyed for ever. Scientists around the world are experimenting with spraying ancient wooden ships with alkaline solutions, to neutralise the sulphuric acid. We hope they are successful.

- When the wreck of the *Mary Rose* was lifted, approximately what proportion of the wreck was wood and what proportion was sea water?

- Why do you think the programme to spray the *Mary Rose* with polyethylene glycol wax takes 10 years?

- Explain in your own words where the hydrogen sulphide in the wood came from.

- Explain in your own words how the polyethylene glycol wax is helping preserve ancient ships, and also how it is contributing to their decay.

Activities

- Archaeologists always worry about whether ancient artefacts should be moved or left where they are found. They decided to lift the *Mary Rose* because the wreck would have been destroyed had it been left where it was. Discuss what things could damage or destroy an ancient underwater shipwreck.

- Do some research to find out more about the *Mary Rose*. Can you find out about any other materials, other than wood, found on board the ship? Can you find out how they are being preserved?

Don't over-react

You know that metals react with water and oxygen. Some metals, such as sodium or potassium, react very quickly in the laboratory, but even iron, that hardly seems to react at all in the laboratory, will soon rust away outside. So how do you choose the right metal? These experts explain how they choose suitable metals for the things they make.

I am a jeweller, and I know just how important it is to choose the right metal. People wear their favourite pieces of jewellery for years and years. The last thing they want is for it to go rusty or black if it gets sweat on it. They want it to come up clean and shiny when they wash it with water, or when they rub it with a soft cloth. So it's very important for me to use metals that don't react with air or water, or with the chemicals in sweat. Lots of jewellery is made from silver, or even steel or copper covered with silver for very cheap jewellery, but silver goes black too quickly for me. It reacts with air and water to make a layer of black silver oxide that you have to keep cleaning off. I only make gold and platinum jewellery. It is much more expensive to buy, but it stays looking as good as the day you bought it, because gold and platinum just don't react with anything. Pure gold is a bit soft and in time it starts to look scratched, so most gold jewellery is made from gold mixed with other metals to make it a bit harder. The other metals also mean you can get gold jewellery that is white, gold or even red coloured!

I work for a company that makes mobile phones, and we use gold all the time. Have you got one of those phones with rectangular connectors that look like two rows of little teeth? The 'teeth' are gold. The connectors are so small that if the metal they are made from reacted with water in the air, and got a layer of corrosion on it, it wouldn't make good contact any more and your phone wouldn't work properly. So we cover the connectors with a very thin layer of gold that doesn't react with air or water.

I am an orthopaedic surgeon. I work with bones. I repair very badly broken bones, such as those people might have after a motorbike accident. If a bone has been badly broken into lots of pieces, my job is a bit like a jigsaw puzzle. I have to put all the pieces of bone back in the right places and hold them together with metal plates and screws. Sometimes I have to put in metal plates to replace bits of bone that I can't find. It wouldn't do to use just any old metal that would go rusty inside the person and make them ill. I have to use a metal that won't react with blood or other body fluids, and that is strong enough to hold the bits of bone in place while they heal. The metal I use is titanium, because it doesn't react with anything. It is twice as strong as steel and much lighter than steel. Titanium is also used in aeroplanes and aeroplane engines because it is so light and strong.

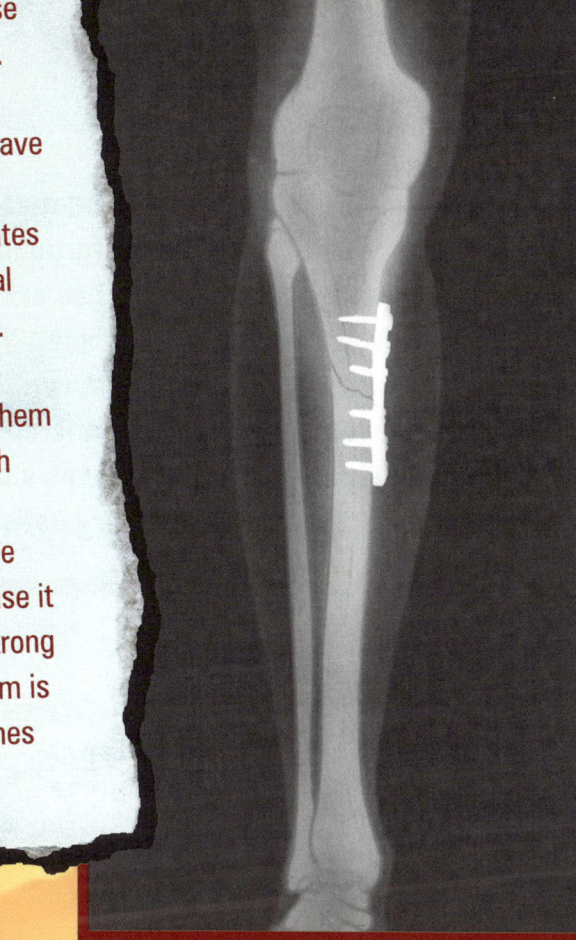

Qs

○ List three metals that don't react with air or water.

○ Why does silver jewellery get a black layer on it?

○ Why does pure gold usually have other metals mixed with it, to make jewellery?

○ What is an orthopaedic surgeon?

○ Give two reasons why orthopaedic surgeons use bone screws and plates made from titanium.

— Activities —

■ Discuss why it is important to hold all the broken pieces of bone in the right places while they heal. What might happen if they weren't held in the right places?

■ Design a short (30 seconds or less) radio advertisement telling young teenagers of the dangers of riding motorbikes.

Worthless treasure?

Archaeologists like finding ancient metal objects because they don't rot away underground like cloth, leather or wood does, and they are easy to preserve; you just clean them and keep them dry. So when the first metal objects recovered from shipwrecks looked like lumps of concrete, and fell apart when they were dried out, it was a bit disappointing. Our expert explains what's going on.

Setting the scene

Different metals, different places

You already know that most metals corrode, but some corrode much faster than others. We expect iron to go rusty quite quickly, but we would be very surprised if a gold ring corroded. You probably know that how quickly a metal reacts with air and water depends on where it is in the reactivity series; metals that are higher up the reactivity series react, and so corrode, faster. How fast metals corrode also depends on their environment. The moisture and salts in sea water make iron corrode five times faster than it would in soil, and ten times faster than it would in air. That's why metal things don't last as well under sea water as they do buried in soil.

What about the concrete?

It isn't really concrete, though it can be as hard as concrete. Archaeologists call it 'encrustation' because it forms a hard crust round the metal object. Sea water doesn't only have salt (sodium chloride) dissolved in it, it has lots of other dissolved minerals as well. As a metal object corrodes in sea water, the chemicals produced change the pH value of the sea water. This stops the sea water being able to dissolve some chemicals, such as calcium carbonate, and they settle out (precipitate) around the metal object. The chemicals mix with sand and marine bacteria to make the hard, concrete-like coating usually found on metal objects from ancient shipwrecks. Archaeologists usually have to remove the encrustation using a hammer and chisel or a sandblaster. It does come off fairly easily though, so the metal object underneath is not damaged.

Why do they fall apart in air, when they were alright underwater?

It's all to do with oxygen. The chemical reactions that form the layer of corrosion need oxygen from the sea water. As the layer of corrosion builds up on the metal, it gets harder and harder for oxygen from the sea water to reach the metal object and the corrosion reactions slow down, or even stop. When the object is taken out of sea water into the air, a different set of chemical reactions starts to happen. The chemicals in the layer of corrosion react with oxygen in the air. The new chemicals made take up more space than the original corrosion chemicals did, so bits of the layer of corrosion start to expand, and force the rest apart. Often the corrosion has got deep into the metal object through cracks in the metal too fine to see, so the whole metal object falls apart. Sometimes iron cannons have even exploded!

The *Mary Rose* sank in 1545. Metal objects found on board included cannons, gold coins, mugs and plates, and even a doctor's syringe.

So do we have to just leave metal objects underwater then?

No, but they have to be kept in special solutions that keep out the oxygen, until they have been cleaned. Chlorine in the sea water reacts with the metal to make metal chlorides as well. When the objects are brought to the surface, these metal chlorides react to form hydrochloric acid that makes the corrosion worse, so the objects are kept in alkaline solutions to neutralise the acid.

Qs

- Give two reasons why metal objects corrode at different rates.

- What do archaeologists call the concrete-like layer that forms round metal objects in sea water?

- How does the corrosion get into the metal object itself, and why can this make the object fall apart when it is taken out of the sea water?

- Describe two ways that the special solutions protect metal objects until they are cleaned.

Activities

- Archaeologists always worry about whether or not they should dig something up; they might damage it and future archaeologists might have been able to care for it better. Imagine you are an archaeologist, and discuss the things that would help you decide whether to dig something up or leave it where it is.

- Use the internet to find pictures of objects recovered from the *Mary Rose*. Make a scrapbook or PowerPoint presentation.

Reacting strangely!

Setting the scene

You have learned how some metals combine with oxygen or with acids, to form compounds, much more easily than other metals do. You have probably drawn a reactivity series to show how well different metals react. However the way we are able to use some metals doesn't seem to fit with their position in the reactivity series. Read this science magazine page to find out why not.

*New*Science Magazine

The reactivity series

The reactivity series is one of the pieces of information scientists and engineers use when deciding which metals are suitable for particular purposes. For example, platinum and gold do not form oxides in the air, so they are suitable for making jewellery since they stay bright and shiny without cleaning. Titanium is both low on the reactivity series and very strong, so it is suitable for places where steel machinery would corrode very quickly, such as in sea water.

Aluminium aircraft

Aluminium is a surprising metal. It's very light, so it is commonly used for building things such as aircraft, but it is also high on the reactivity series, well above iron and copper and nearly as reactive as magnesium. According to the reactivity series, aluminium aircraft should disintegrate rapidly when exposed to air or rain, but they don't! The reason is that although aluminium is highly reactive, aluminium oxide isn't. So in air, aluminium is rapidly coated in tough aluminium oxide, which prevents any further corrosion. When aircraft are made, the aluminium undergoes a process called 'anodising' that makes this layer of aluminium oxide thicker to give better protection.

However the layer of aluminium oxide is not completely impermeable. Aircraft passengers are forbidden to carry anything containing mercury in their luggage because mercury reacts vigorously with aluminium oxide. Mercury is a metal that is liquid at room temperature, and is widely used in industry, for making fluorescent lamps, paints, batteries, dental fillings, pesticides, and other things. Mercury reacts with the layer of aluminium oxide and breaks it up. The aluminium underneath is exposed to the air, reacts to form more aluminium oxide, which in turn reacts with the mercury, and so on. Less than a teaspoonful of mercury can produce large holes in an aircraft, causing it to crash.

It's hard to believe that this much mercury could make an aircraft crash, but it's true.

Catalytic converters

Cars and other vehicles give off many polluting gases, including carbon monoxide and nitrogen oxides. Most modern cars now have catalytic converters to change these polluting gases to less harmful ones. The 'active ingredients' in catalytic converters are three of the least reactive metals known, platinum, palladium and rhodium! Hot exhaust gases flow into the catalytic converter, making it extremely hot – hot enough to set grass on fire if a car fitted with a catalytic converter parks in long grass – and making the metals more reactive. Nitrogen atoms from the nitrogen oxide gases react with platinum and rhodium and become 'stuck' to the catalytic converter, while the oxygen is released as oxygen gas. The 'stuck' nitrogen atoms react with other nitrogen atoms on the catalytic converter, forming nitrogen gas that is released. Platinum and palladium trap carbon monoxide molecules and oxygen atoms, that then combine with each other to form carbon dioxide gas, that is released.

Catalytic converters were invented in the 1970s, before scientists knew about global warming, to control polluting gases at ground level. Now many scientists fear that catalytic converters are actually making global warming worse, by releasing large amounts of carbon dioxide gas.

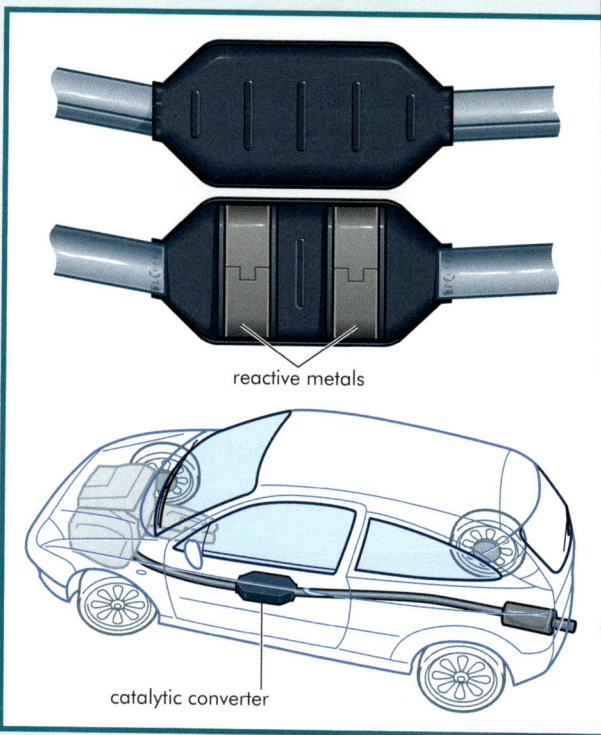

reactive metals

catalytic converter

Catalytic converters mean less pollution at ground level, but do they make global warming worse?

Is pollution getting better or worse?

You have probably learned how burning fossil fuels causes pollution. Perhaps you have heard people on television talking about acid rain or global warming. Both of these are caused by pollution. Sometimes people make it sound like pollution just keeps getting worse. The problem is how can we tell? Scot is an environmental pollution monitor. It's his job to find out if pollution is getting better or worse. So how does he do it?

Interviewer Good morning, Scot. I understand you're going to tell us if pollution is getting worse.

Scot I'm going to do my best.

Interviewer I'm sure I remember reading somewhere that lots of towns used to be covered in black soot all the time from smoky factory chimneys. Isn't it obvious that now pollution is nothing like as bad as that?

Scot There is certainly a lot less sooty smoke than there used to be, but sooty smoke isn't the only type of pollution. There are some types of pollution that you can't even see, but they're still there. My job is to measure lots of different types of pollution and see if the amount is changing.

Interviewer Let me guess! You compare the results you get now with the results people got years and years ago?

Scot Sort of, except that years and years ago people didn't even know some types of pollution existed, and they didn't measure any pollution.

Interviewer Good gracious, so what can you do?

Scot There's still a lot of evidence I can use. Sometimes I use people's diaries and doctors' notes about what illnesses people had. Sometimes wood from old trees or bits of plants buried in the soil tell me about how well trees and plants were growing. Some types of pollution stop plants growing well, or even make some plants grow better!

This moth tells scientists about pollution. Some of the moths are black and some are white. When tree trunks are black and sooty there are more of the black moths because they don't show up against the tree trunk and birds don't eat them.

Interviewer And what evidence do you collect today?

Scot We collect samples of air and rainwater from all over the country, in lots of different places, in towns and in the countryside. Then we test them for lots of polluting chemicals. Other scientists are doing the same in other countries, and we share our results with each other.

Interviewer So what does the evidence tell you? Is pollution better than it was?

Scot It's still hard to say, because pollution has changed a lot. As you said earlier, there's a lot less smoke and soot in towns, and that's better for people's health. But a lot of pollution goes high into the Earth's atmosphere and gets blown around the world by the wind. It might affect people hundreds of kilometres from where the pollution came from.

Interviewer It doesn't sound very good news.

Scot I didn't mean to sound gloomy. We haven't solved all the problems of pollution yet, but we know so much more about it than we did. And lots of the answers are really beginning to work. Most countries now have tests for cars to measure how much pollution they are giving out, and cars that give out too much are repaired or scrapped. Lots of power stations are using cleaner fuels, or changing to renewable energy resources.

Vehicles that give out pollution like this are repaired or scrapped.

Interviewer So what about the future?

Scot We don't know yet. I think things are getting better, but we mustn't stop working hard to make the whole environment cleaner and healthier for all of us.

Interviewer Well, thank you for that. It's given us a lot to think about.

- Where did one type of pollution come from in towns years ago?

- When Scot measures pollution, why can't he compare his results with results from years and years ago?

- Describe two bits of evidence Scot can use from years ago.

- What does Scot do to find out how much pollution there is today?

- Explain why power stations give out less pollution than they used to.

Activities

- Most of our pollution comes from vehicles and from power stations generating electricity. Discuss some of the things we can do to try to reduce the amount of pollution we cause.

- Imagine you work in a garage, repairing cars. Role-play the conversation you have with an angry car driver whose car has just failed a pollution test. Explain to him why the pollution test is important and why he has to have his car repaired.

Acid rain – what happens next?

You know that burning fossil fuels causes acid rain and you probably know how acid rain can damage buildings, living things and the environment. We tend to think of acid rain as a modern problem, but we have been burning large amounts of coal for hundreds of years. So why did it take so long to find out about acid rain, and how close are we to solving all the problems it causes?

Setting the scene

Question: *If acid rain is caused by burning fossil fuels, why didn't the acid rain problems start when we first started burning large amounts of coal, in the 18th and 19th centuries?*

Answer: They did. Scientists first noticed them in the 17th century, but for hundreds of years they thought it was only a small problem close to smoky industries. They did not realise it was a serious international problem until the 1960s when fishermen noticed fish numbers dropping, and some species disappearing in lakes in North America hundreds of kilometres from any industries. Even then, it took time and lots of research to find out what was causing the damage to the lakes.

Question: *Why didn't scientists start solving the acid rain problems straight away?*

Answer: The acid rain problems are caused by thousands of industries in many different countries, and by millions of people, including us, around the world. They are problems that we have all caused, and we all have to solve them. Scientists cannot solve the problems; they can only advise governments about how to solve the problems. The governments then have to compare the cost of the problems caused by acid rain with the cost of solving the problems, and decide what to do. It took many years for governments around the world to agree on solutions that would probably work and that would not be too expensive.

Question: *I've heard that governments around the world have agreed on laws to decrease the amount of polluting gases that industries and vehicles give out. Does that mean that acid rain isn't a problem any more?*

Answer: Scientists aren't quite sure yet. They don't know if laws would decrease the amount of polluting gases enough for the environment to recover. They need to keep collecting evidence to show how much effect the decrease in polluting gases is having. Also some of the acid rain problems are caused by 'dry acid deposition' – dry particles that settle out and become acidic when they dissolve in dew or rainwater. Scientists aren't sure how much effect dry acid deposition has because the exact amount of dry acid deposition is very difficult to measure.

Question: *How long will it take for environments damaged by acid rain to recover completely?*

Answer: We don't know that either. So far scientists have been a bit disappointed by how slowly some environments seem to be recovering. They think it might be because important minerals have been dissolved out of the soil by acid rain, and washed away. So the soil has been left with less minerals for plant growth and with less minerals to neutralise acid rain still falling on the soil. They fear that it may take tens or even hundreds of years for some environments to recover, but they are not sure.

Scientists are trying to find out why forests like this are taking longer to recover than they expected, even when the acid rain has decreased.

- When did scientists first realise that acid rain was a serious international problem?

- Why did governments take a long time to decide what to do about acid rain problems?

- Explain in your own words one reason why scientists aren't sure whether the environment is recovering from acid rain problems.

- Describe a possible reason why some environments seem to be recovering more slowly than scientists expected.

Activities

- Discuss some of the ways you could change your lifestyle, so that you used less energy, helping burn less fossil fuels, and helping solve the acid rain problem.

- Do some research. Most of the gases that cause acid rain are given out by industry or by vehicles. Find out more about one way that is used to decrease the amount of these gases given out.

Carbon and global warming

You know that extra carbon dioxide in the atmosphere, from burning fossil fuels, is causing global warming. You may have heard many different estimates of how much the world will warm up, and how long it will take, but have you ever wondered why scientists seem unable to work out the effect global warming will have? Reese and Benson have been looking at science magazine articles to try to find out.

Climate change killed the dinosaurs

In the 1980s, scientists first suggested that the dinosaurs were killed by climate change. They found evidence of a huge asteroid hitting Earth at about the time dinosaurs went extinct. The idea was that the asteroid impact threw so much dust into the air that it went dark. The Sun's rays couldn't get through, making it cold and dark; plants stopped growing and the dinosaurs died of cold or starved. Recent evidence from fossil plants shows this idea might be wrong. The fossil plants have fewer pores than normal on their leaves, suggesting that it was easier for them to absorb carbon dioxide because there was more carbon dioxide in the air. Now scientists think that perhaps the asteroid impact changed carbonate rocks into gas, making the amount of carbon dioxide in the atmosphere go up by four or five times. They think that perhaps global warming killed the dinosaurs rather than the Earth getting colder.

Ice and global warming

Satellite surveys show that ice at the North Pole is definitely melting. Some scientists fear this will make global warming worse. The Earth will warm up as dark coloured land and sea water absorbs more of the Sun's energy than the light coloured ice did. Other surveys show that the warmer temperatures are making more snow fall in the Antarctic and the amount of ice there is increasing, making global warming slow down. In 2002, American scientists surveying underwater ice near the Arctic, reported that large holes were forming in the ice. They fear that as the ice melts, billions of tonnes of carbon trapped in the ice will be released, increasing the amount of carbon dioxide in the atmosphere and making global warming worse.

Computer model solves global warming problem

Scientists in Norway have built a computer model to show what happens to waste carbon dioxide gas. Their model shows that if we turned the waste carbon dioxide gas into a liquid and pumped it into the ocean, 800 metres down, it would dissolve in the sea water, then sink. It would stay trapped for centuries because water with dissolved carbon dioxide in it is heavier than water with less carbon dioxide.

18

I still like the idea of the dinosaurs dying out because it went cold and dark and plants stopped growing.

I suppose that's why scientists keep looking for more evidence even when they think they've got the right answer. Sometimes new evidence shows that an old idea might be wrong, even when it seems like a really clever idea. I'm glad they've solved the problem of how to stop global warming though.

It's only a computer model. They don't know if it's really right yet.

Qs

- What evidence did scientists find to suggest that the idea that an asteroid impact stopped plants growing was wrong?

- Describe what may have happened to the carbon released when an asteroid hit Earth. Use diagrams or pictures if you want to.

- Describe in your own words how changing the amount of ice on the Earth's surface may affect the Earth's temperature.

- The computer model for pumping carbon dioxide into the ocean does not take into account the fuel needed to liquefy and pump the waste carbon dioxide gas. How might this affect whether or not the idea would solve the problem of global warming?

Activities

- Imagine you are an international team of government scientists trying to decide what evidence to collect to find out if global warming is getting better or worse, and if any of the measures governments have introduced so far are working. Role-play the discussion you will have.

- Design a poster to illustrate one of the scientific ideas mentioned in the article. Use research to find out more about your chosen idea, if you wish.

Recycling plastic

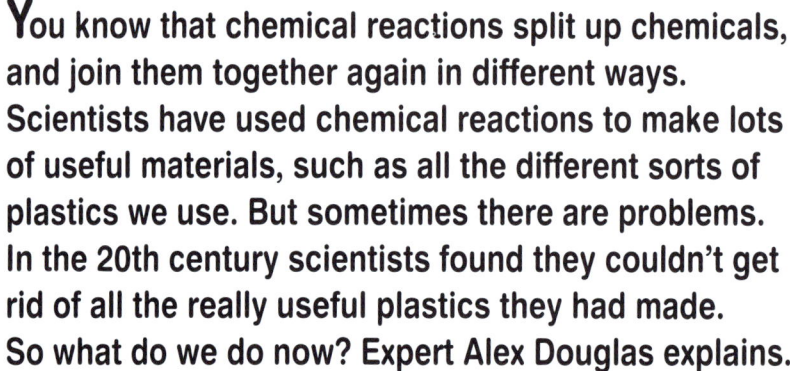

Setting the scene

You know that chemical reactions split up chemicals, and join them together again in different ways. Scientists have used chemical reactions to make lots of useful materials, such as all the different sorts of plastics we use. But sometimes there are problems. In the 20th century scientists found they couldn't get rid of all the really useful plastics they had made. So what do we do now? Expert Alex Douglas explains.

Interviewer Hello, Alex. I thought plastics were really useful. Are you telling us that they aren't useful after all?

Alex No, certainly not. Plastics are very, very useful. The different plastics scientists have made are much better than the materials people used to use. There are soft, bendy ones, strong, hard ones, ones that won't burn or scratch and lots more. But once plastics have been made, it is difficult to get rid of them because they don't rot or rust like other materials do.

Interviewer Does that matter? Why can't we just recycle them? People say recycling is good for the environment.

Alex That's right, it is. The problem is that plastics are very hard to recycle.

Interviewer You mean people just throw them away instead of collecting them?

Alex It's not that. It's that there are so many types of plastic and they all look nearly the same, even though they're not. If you just melted down lots of different sorts of plastic and then set it again into new plastic objects, they would be useless. The plastic would be weak and break. You have to keep each type of plastic by itself – but people can't tell them apart!

Interviewer So can't we recycle any plastic?

Alex Yes, some of the ideas people have had are brilliant. Do you ever wear fleece jumpers or jackets? They are made from recycled plastic drinks bottles! Sometimes recycled plastic cups are made into pencils or pens.

Interviewer What about other things made from plastic? What happens to them?

Alex   Soon we might be able to recycle all plastics. Some scientists in Italy have found a way to make a strong, useful plastic from two different types of plastic. Plastic is made from very long chains of thousands of atoms all joined together. The Italian scientists grind the plastic up into a fine powder and them mix it with very cold, liquid, carbon dioxide. There are lots of tiny explosions as the carbon dioxide warms up and turns back into a gas, and these explosions split the long chains of atoms into lots of short chains. The short chains mix up and join together again to make a new, strong plastic. The Italian scientists hope that soon they will be able to make new plastics like this, using any type of plastic to start with.

Interviewer   When I was last shopping, my supermarket said its plastic shopping bags were biodegradable. Does that mean they can be recycled?

Alex   It means that they will rot down, just like paper or wood does, but they take a bit longer. Lots and lots of plastic things have been thrown away, and will stay buried in landfill sites for ever more. But if these new, biodegradable bags are thrown away in landfill sites they will rot down and disappear, so it's a good thing.

Interviewer   So why didn't scientists always make plastic biodegradable then?

Alex   They couldn't. They have only just found out how to. We are always finding out more, you know!

Interviewer   Well, I've certainly found out a lot more about plastic. Thank you for talking to us, Alex.

Biodegradable

Biodegradable

100% biodegradable – helping the environment every time you shop

Qs

- In the 20th century, what was the problem scientists found with plastics?

- Why is it no good to just melt down old plastic and make it into new plastic objects?

- What are some of the things that have been made from recycled plastic objects?

- What do the Italian scientists mix powdered plastic with to break up the long chains of atoms? How does it work?

- Why are biodegradable plastic bags better than non-biodegradable ones?

Activities

- Even when plastics can be recycled or when they are biodegradable, many scientists still think it is better for us and for the environment if we use less plastics. Discuss some of the things you could do, to use less plastic.

- Do some research to find out how plastics have changed. Ask some elderly people what plastics were like when they were children. Ask questions like: What sorts of things were made from plastic? Did toys made from plastic last well? and so on.

Challenger Space Shuttle

You have learned that when we burn fuels, chemical reactions happen and we get useful energy. You know that not all fuels are the same – it would be dangerous to put petrol on your living room fire or on a bonfire, because it burns far more fiercely than wood or coal and gives out far more energy. But space travel needs fuel that gives out even more energy than petrol. So what are the dangers connected with rocket fuel?

28th January 1986

SEVEN DIE IN SPACE SHUTTLE DISASTER

Millions of Americans watched in horror today as the American Space Shuttle *Challenger* exploded just 73 seconds after lift-off, killing all seven astronauts on board. The launch was being shown live on TV, and the families of the seven astronauts were watching from the Kennedy Space Centre. One of the astronauts was the 37-year old school teacher, Christa McAuliffe, who would have been the first civilian in space. Scientists are already looking for clues to find out why the disaster happened. The American President has praised the courage and bravery of the seven astronauts.

Read these imaginary diary entries to find out how the scientists solved the problem of what happened.

FEBRUARY 1986

I have been put on the team of scientists finding out why the Challenger Space Shuttle exploded. I am excited, but a bit scared too. It's more than just a science problem. I know the families are really hoping we can tell them why their loved ones died. And we have so little evidence to use – there wasn't much wreckage left, most of it burned up. Still we have got two clues that should help.

Clue 1: We know it was very cold at the launch site.

Clue 2: We've got a film of the launch showing black smoke coming from a joint at the bottom of the booster rocket. That's the rocket that spacecraft like *Challenger* have to give them a bit of extra 'push' to help them get up into space. Once they're in space the booster rocket drops off and they move around using an engine that runs on hydrogen fuel, with oxygen to make the hydrogen burn.

MAY 1986

At last we know exactly why *Challenger* blew up. We worked it out by looking at the film, guessing what was happening, predicting what would happen next if our guess was right, then looking back to the film to see if our prediction was right.

We now know that the black smoke was because a seal had cracked in the cold weather. Fuel and hot gas from the booster rocket leaked out and burned through the supports that held the booster rocket on. We could see the flames on the film of the disaster. The booster rocket came loose too early and split the tanks of liquid hydrogen and liquid oxygen. We know the tanks were split because the film showed a cloud of white gas round *Challenger*. That was the hydrogen and oxygen vapour, leaking from the split tanks. Then the hydrogen and oxygen caught alight and exploded, blowing *Challenger* up and killing all the astronauts.

What next you might ask? We have to re-design and re-test the fuel seals at the joints to make sure this can't happen again.

The families of the dead astronauts have formed a group called the Challenger Organisation. They want to build lots of educational centres around the world where students can learn about space and space travel. We have to help them.

Qs

- When did the *Challenger* accident happen?

- What was the most useful evidence for the scientists finding out why the accident happened?

- What happened after a fuel seal cracked in the cold weather?

- What does the *Challenger* disaster tell you about the burning reaction of hydrogen and oxygen?

- Do you think hydrogen would burn more or less fiercely in air than in oxygen? Give a reason.

— Activities —

- Some people say space travel is far too dangerous to send people into space, but only about 20 astronauts have ever died in over 30 years of space travel. Compare this with more than 3000 deaths in road accidents every year in the UK. Discuss what you think about the safety of space travel.

- Most of us don't have to deal with fuels as dangerous as rocket fuel. But people such as firemen or garage mechanics have to deal with containers of fuel or gases that might explode. Find out some more about what they do to make the dangers as small as possible.

Life on Venus?

Have you ever wondered whether there are living things elsewhere in the Universe, other than on Earth? People have probably wondered if there is 'anyone out there' since we first looked up at the stars. Astronomers have used telescopes to look for light or radio signals coming from other planets, but what if the life forms are not advanced enough to send out signals? Chemistry is helping in the search for other clues.

Setting the scene

Interviewer Today I'm talking to Matt, an astronomer, who's going to tell us about an exciting new discovery on Venus.

Matt Hello. That's right. We were studying the atmosphere around Venus when we found something really interesting.

Interviewer Do you mean you sent astronauts to Venus to see what was there?

Matt No, we haven't even sent a spacecraft.

Interviewer You've lost me. How can you tell what the atmosphere is like then?

Matt We look at the radiation coming from Venus. Radio telescopes detect the heat radiation and that tells us how hot Venus is. Other telescopes detect the reflected sunlight from Venus and that tells us what chemicals are there.

Interviewer Really? How?

Matt Particles of gas in the atmosphere absorb and reflect the sunlight. Normally sunlight is made up of lots of different colours of light, just like those you see if you split the light up with a prism. Different chemicals absorb and reflect different colours of light, so by looking at the colours of light coming from Venus we can tell what chemicals are in Venus's atmosphere. We can even tell how much of each of the different chemicals there are.

Interviewer That's really clever. So what did Venus's atmosphere tell you?

Matt We were particularly interested in Venus because our studies had shown that there is water in the atmosphere around Venus. Living things on Earth need water, so we thought that if there is water around Venus perhaps there are living things there as well.

Venus has a temperature of about 400°C. Is it really possible that there might be life on Venus?

54

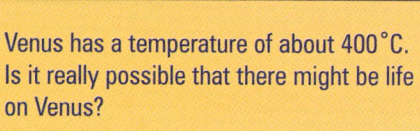

Interviewer And are there?

Matt We don't know, but there might be. We would have expected lots of carbon monoxide around Venus, because ultra-violet light from the Sun usually makes carbon monoxide, from carbon and oxygen that we know are present. It is almost as though something is removing the carbon monoxide.

Interviewer Could it be a coincidence?

Matt Possibly, but we have also detected hydrogen sulphide and sulphur dioxide. It's very rare to find these gases together because they react with each other. We think they are only there because something keeps making them as fast as they react together.

Interviewer Are you saying there are living things on the surface of Venus?

Matt No, not on the surface. But we think there are microbes living in the water vapour surrounding Venus.

Interviewer But I thought Venus was really hot. Wouldn't they get cooked?

Matt The surface of Venus is really hot. But at about 50 kilometres up, the atmosphere is only about 70°C. We think microbes could survive there, and use ultra-violet light from the Sun as an energy source.

Interviewer So how can you tell if you are right?

Matt We hope that in 2005 a 'Venus Express' spacecraft will be launched to travel to Venus to collect a sample of the atmosphere and bring it back for us to study.

The atmosphere around Venus must be a bit like the steam from this hot spring. Perhaps the first life on Earth evolved in conditions like this, too.

Qs

- What two types of radiation from Venus do astronomers study?

- How can they detect the presence of different chemicals in the atmosphere of Venus?

- Which two gases make the presence of microbes in the atmosphere of Venus most likely? Why?

- All living things need energy. What do scientists think microbes around Venus might be using as an energy source? Can you think of any other sources of energy that you know are available?

Activities

- Not all scientists believe there could be life in the atmosphere of Venus; some say a large amount of water would be needed to support life, not just water droplets. It has been suggested that Venus was once cool and wet, but then suffered serious 'global warming'. Discuss whether this would make life in the atmosphere of Venus more or less likely.

- Role-play the discussion that might take place between astronomers studying the atmosphere of Venus and Space Agency officials. The astronomers must try to convince the Space Agency officials that it would be worth sending a spacecraft to Venus to collect a sample of the atmosphere for study.

Clockwork computers?

Setting the scene

We use electricity every day. In our homes and schools, we just flick a switch and there is electricity for lights, fridges, televisions, computer games, and much more. Businesses use electricity to keep in touch with each other using telephones and email. Can you imagine life without electricity? This article describes some new ways that are being used to generate electricity in developing countries, where people do not have mains electricity.

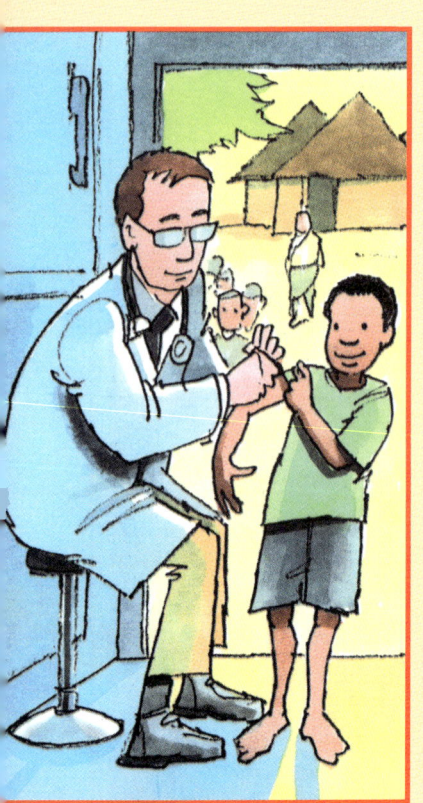

These vaccines have to be kept cold – and you need electricity for the fridges.

About two billion of the poorest people in the world do not have any electricity – that's about one third of the world's population. If they had electricity, they could use fridges to store medicines and vaccines. They could use radios and telephones to communicate with the rest of the world. Electricity could run small machines, so the people could make items to sell. The money they make would pay for schools, hospitals, clean water, and seeds and animals for community farms. But they cannot afford to build power stations with wires to carry the electricity to hundreds of small villages. Batteries are too expensive as well, and the nearest town where they could buy them is often several days' walk away. Fortunately, the energy to make electricity can be found in some novel ways!

Solar-powered lights

You may have seen solar-powered lights in garden centres. They run on electricity generated from the energy in sunlight, and stored in a battery until it gets dark. We buy solar-powered lights because they look nice, but they are really helping many people in developing countries. In countries near the equator it gets dark at about 6.30 pm every evening. Solar-powered lights are much safer than the smoky candles and oil lamps people used to use. They allow families to work and earn money for longer each day; and they allow children to do school work and become educated, so they can earn more money. Electricity generated from the energy in sunlight is also being used to run fridges, so medicines can be stored and food stays fresh for longer so less of it is wasted.

You're winding me up!

In the early 1990s, a British engineer called Trevor Baylis invented a clockwork radio. It has a tiny electricity generator inside, just like the electricity generator in a power station but much, much smaller. You turn a handle to wind up a spring inside, just like a clockwork toy. Then the spring turns the tiny generator to generate a small amount of electricity to make the radio work. The first clockwork radio had to be wound up for 30 seconds to make the radio work for about 30 minutes. Since then, Trevor has made his radio smaller and lighter, and it works for longer after you wind it up. He has also made clockwork torches, clockwork mobile phones and even clockwork computers. The latest clockwork radios and computers have a rechargeable battery inside them. When you turn the handle, the electricity generator charges up the battery, so that you can use the radio or computer for hours without having to wind it again. Trevor's most recent inventions include a clockwork-powered laser beam for eye surgery and a clockwork-powered landmine detector.

Clockwork radios, phones and computers let people in remote areas keep in touch with the rest of the world.

Qs

- How many people in the world don't have any electricity?

- Describe two ways in which electricity would make their life better.

- Explain how solar lights help these people.

- Who invented the clockwork radio, and when?

- List some other clockwork-powered things Trevor has invented.

Activities

- Try to imagine that you live in a poor, rural village without any electricity. Discuss what would be important to you. If your village were given a way to generate electricity, what would you most like to use the electricity to do? Why?

- Use the internet to find out some more about Trevor Baylis, the man who invented the clockwork radio.

Sporting electricity

Setting the scene

When you think about new inventions, you probably think of very clever, complicated things such as laptop computers, interactive television, medical equipment or space-age technology. But inventions don't have to be like that. Some inventions use relatively simple science in a new way that nobody else has thought of. Read Ahmed's journal about his skiing trip with his school to find out more.

MONDAY

We got 'kitted out' this morning with all the right clothing and skis that are the right size – I never really thought about it before but heavier people get longer skis so they don't sink into the snow. The speed you ski at has something to do with it as well, but the man said that as we are beginners we don't have to worry about that! Then we went out onto this really shallow slope and practised starting and stopping. I didn't fall over once!

TUESDAY

We went onto a much longer slope today. I was scared of just getting faster and faster and not being able to stop, but our instructor said not to worry about that – our skis have all got brakes! I've never heard of brakes on skis before, but apparently they're a new idea, only invented about a year ago by an engineer from America. Each ski has a small box on it with a battery inside. The battery is connected to metal on the underside of the ski and to a speed sensor. If you go too fast, the current switches on and the metal acts as a brake. I don't see how it can, but I forgot to ask. Anyway, I know they work because just as I was getting a bit nervous because I was speeding up, the brakes came on and slowed me down. Inside the box with the battery there's a little lever you can move to change the speed when the brakes switch on.

WEDNESDAY

I turned up the speed on my ski brakes today. So I must be getting better at skiing! I'm still one of the slowest in my group though. I found out how the brakes work today, as well. There's a thin piece of metal which runs along each side of the bottom of the ski, with more pieces of metal running across the ski from each long strip, a bit like the teeth of a comb. The bottom of the ski looks like it's got two metal 'combs' on it, with the teeth interlocking, but not quite touching. Each 'comb' is attached to opposite sides of the battery, so when the brakes are switched on, one 'comb' gets a positive electric charge on it and the other 'comb' gets a negative electric charge on it. The snow gets attracted to these charges, so the friction gets greater and the ski slows down. The 'teeth' of the 'combs' are also close enough together for a small current to flow through the snow from one 'comb' to the other. This current makes a tiny bit of the snow melt briefly and as it refreezes it sticks to the ski. That increases the friction too, helping me to slow down. It's really clever!

metal

battery

underside of ski

Qs

- Why do people of different weights have different lengths of skis?

- What does the speed sensor switch on, to make the ski brakes work?

- Describe how the electric charges on the metal 'combs' on the skis help to increase the friction.

- Explain how the current is used to help increase friction.

Activities

- The ski brakes switch on when the speed sensor detects that the ski is going too fast. Ahmed wondered if it would be better to have a switch, so he could switch the brakes on whenever he wanted to. Which do you think would be better and why? Do you think it would be better if some skiers had a switch to switch on the brakes and some skis had brakes that came on on their own?

- Are the new ski brakes really useful or are they just a 'gimmick'? Design a questionnaire that the inventor could send to ski resorts and hospitals to find out if the new ski brakes really do help prevent beginner skiers having accidents.

Better than batteries

Most of the electricity you use probably comes from the mains or from batteries. These both have disadvantages; mains electricity is not portable, batteries are expensive and 'go flat' quickly. How have scientists overcome these problems to make electricity available in new situations, and to make it accessible to huge sections of the world's population who were unable to use it before?

Setting the scene

FOR ALL YOUR OUTDOOR NEEDS

We are your biggest local stockist of outdoor leisure goods. Last year's best seller, the Outdoor Solar Lamp is on special offer this month, with a 25% discount. This year's new model contains a larger solar cell and an improved battery, to store that sunlight for even longer, so your lamp will stay on all evening! New for this year is the amazing 'Wind-up Phone Charger'. No it's not a wind-up – just turn the handle for a few seconds and the charger will charge your phone battery enough to give you up to five minutes' conversation time.

WIND CONES –
the Safe, Eco-friendly Road Cone

The Wind Cone is the Ultimate in Roadworks Safety!

Never again will the lights on top of your road cones go out because the battery has gone flat or been nicked! Our road cone comes complete with its own small wind turbine. Wind, or air turbulence from passing vehicles, turns the wind turbine to drive a small electricity generator to light the lamp. Any extra electrical energy generated charges up a rechargeable battery, which keeps the lamp shining even when the air is still.

HEAT AND LIGHT!

The thermoelectric generator uses waste heat to generate electricity. It works on the same principle as an electronic thermometer, but in reverse. Inside the generator is a grid of thermocouples, that can be placed next to a cooker, or furnace or other heat source. Each thermocouple is a loop made from two different metals – ours uses bismuth telluride and aluminium. When the junctions of the two metals are kept at different temperatures an electric current flows in the loop of wire. Our thermoelectric generator adds together all the currents from each thermocouple in the grid to provide enough electricity to power a light bulb or small television.

THERMO-PANELS

Our thermo-panels use state-of-the-art technology called thermophotovoltaics.

They work a bit like a solar cell to generate electricity, but the energy source is heat energy instead of light energy. Heat energy falls onto a special panel called an emitter, which absorbs the energy and re-radiates it as light energy, a bit like the gas mantle on a gas camping lamp. A special filter then transmits the light with the right amount of energy onto a solar cell, which generates electricity, and reflects the rest of the light back to the emitter. Thermo-panels are ideal where there is a lot of wasted heat energy, such as near cookers, furnaces or engines.

They generate enough electricity to run lights, or charge telephone or computer batteries.

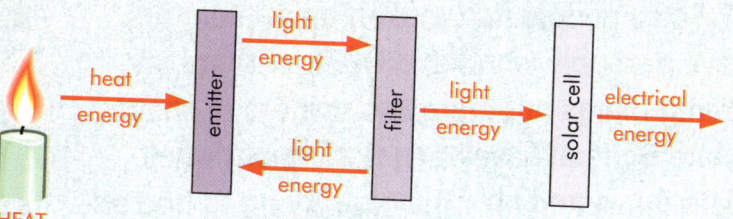

MUSIC AND MOVEMENT!

Ever wanted to power your CD player or MP3 player just by walking along? Now you can! Our electricity can be generated from any kind of vibration or movement! It contains special flexible strips of a 'piezoelectric' material called lead zirconate titanate. Stretching or compressing the flexible strips generates a voltage across the surface of the lead zirconate titanate, just like a small battery.

Qs

- One of the advertisements claims that the Outdoor Solar Lamp has an improved battery 'to store that sunlight for even longer'. Explain what is wrong with this claim.

- 'Piezo' comes from the Greek word for 'push'. Describe in your own words what you think a 'piezoelectric' material is.

- The thermoelectric generator is described as an 'electronic thermometer in reverse'. Suggest how an electronic thermometer works.

- Draw an energy transfer diagram to show the main energy transformations taking place in a thermo-panel.

Activities

- Do you think that the types of electricity generator mentioned here will ever replace our National Grid? Discuss reasons why, or why not.

- Choose one of the types of electricity generator mentioned. Design an informative letter/leaflet that charities can send out appealing for money to help supply this type of electricity generator to small communities in developing countries. Include some of the things that your chosen type of electricity generator might make possible for these communities.

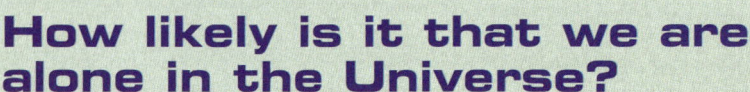

Are we alone?

> Have you ever watched films or read books about aliens? Since people first looked up at the stars, they have probably wondered whether there are other living things out there somewhere in space. Reese and Benson have been finding out what scientists think, and how they are trying to find out.

Setting the scene

How likely is it that we are alone in the Universe?

No one really knows. Some people say that there are so many billions of stars like our Sun that it must be almost certain that there's another planet somewhere, just like Earth, with living organisms on it. Others say that life evolving was so unlikely that it probably only happened once – here.

What is SETI?

The **S**earch for **E**xtra**t**errestrial **I**ntelligence uses telescopes to look for signs of life from elsewhere in the Universe. Intelligent life forms might be sending out signals on purpose, because they are searching for other life forms, just like we are. Some of our technology, such as the microwaves and radio waves we use for communications, leaks out into space all the time. Another life form with technology similar to ours might be doing the same, sending out signals by accident.

SETI uses telescopes like these all around the world to search for signs from space.

How do scientists know where to look?

We have to look in the right places to find other life forms! Some scientists search for life in new conditions on Earth. They have found bacteria in places where they thought life was impossible, such as tens of metres down under the ice of the Antarctic, and near underwater volcanoes where the water temperature is 400°C. All the living things we have found so far need water, so other scientists search for places in our Solar System where there might be water, or where there was water once. Some think there might have been life on Mars once; others think there may be life now in the vapour clouds around Venus.

What would aliens be like, if they exist?

'Aliens' are most likely to be bacteria. They might be hard to spot because even bacteria on Earth come in many shapes and sizes. So scientists at NASA are developing a computer program that looks at all the micro-organisms we know and spots patterns that only exist in living things. When the program is complete, they hope it will be able to recognise the remains of living things in samples of rocks or gases from other planets in our Solar System.

Robots like these are used to collect samples from planets, for scientists to study back on Earth. But they have to land safely first!

Do you think there are other living things somewhere?

I don't know. I sort of feel that if there were, scientists would have found some evidence of it by now.

I see what you mean, but scientists keep finding more evidence of places where there might be water. A few years ago, they couldn't even do that. Perhaps they've not found anything because their equipment wasn't good enough until now.

What if they keep looking and still don't find anything?

I don't know. There's a lot of space out there! How long do you think it will take them to search all of it?

Qs

- What do the letters SETI stand for?

- Describe how other intelligent life forms might give out signals by accident.

- Why do scientists search for places where there is water, or where there might have been water once?

- List two places in our Solar System, other than Earth, where scientists think there might be life, or might have been life once.

- Explain in your own words why NASA scientists are developing a computer program to look for patterns that only exist in living things.

Activities

- Some people say that scientific research to look for signs of life elsewhere in our Solar System, or in the Universe, is a waste of money. Discuss what you think. Try to explain your reasons.

- If scientists did find evidence of living things elsewhere, how would you feel? Would you be pleased, scared, annoyed, or something else? Can you explain why?

Where r u?

Getting the scene

Today nearly everyone has heard of GPS – you may even know that GPS stands for Global Positioning System. Nearly every camping or 'outdoor leisure' shop has GPS receivers for sale. Yet only ten years ago hardly anyone had heard of GPS. So what is GPS, why has it suddenly become so popular and how does it work? This science magazine page answers some of the most commonly asked questions.

Question:
What is GPS?

Answer:
GPS stands for Global Positioning System. A hand-held GPS receiver, about the size of a mobile phone, picks up signals from satellites orbiting around the Earth, and uses these signals to work out where the GPS receiver is. The position is worked out as an Ordnance Survey grid reference, so if you have a GPS receiver you can tell exactly where you are on your map, often to the nearest 10 metres.

Question:
I know that GPS is getting really popular, but I've never needed one. Who uses it and why?

Answer:
Walkers and sailors mostly, so they know exactly where they are and don't get lost on mountains or at sea. Walkers find a GPS most useful when it's foggy, because then landmarks are invisible and finding the way using a compass gets really difficult. Sailors use a GPS when there are no landmarks because they are out of sight of land. Knowing exactly where you are might make the difference between falling down a cliff and not falling down a cliff, or between running aground on a sandbank and not running aground. Some mobile phones now have GPS in them to help you find your way around, and even to alert emergency services to where you are.

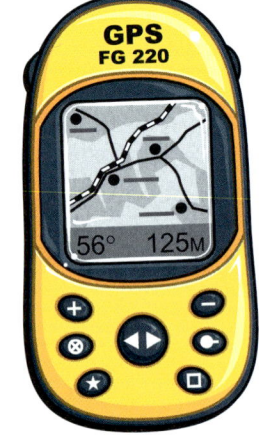

Question:
Who invented the GPS and when?

Answer:
The GPS was developed by the American military in the 1970s, to give them very accurate navigation. In the mid-1990s, they decided that it was so useful that civilians should be able to use it too.

Question:
How does the GPS work?

Answer:

A GPS picks up signals from satellites orbiting the Earth. There are over 20 GPS satellites, each orbiting the Earth twice each day. The satellites are arranged so that from anywhere on Earth a GPS receiver can always 'see' at least four satellites. Each satellite sends out a continuous signal with its own special code and the time. The receiver picks up at least four signals, each telling a slightly different time because each satellite is a different distance away, so each signal takes a slightly different time to arrive. The receiver uses these different times to work out how far away each satellite is, so it can work out where the receiver is.

Question:
Why are there so many GPS satellites?

Answer:

Imagine you know your distance from home. You could be anywhere on a circle. If you know your distance from school as well you could be in one of two places (where the two circles overlap). You need to know your distance from three different places to work out exactly where you are. A fourth distance lets you check the working out is correct. That's why the GPS needs so many satellites, a receiver anywhere on Earth has to be able to detect four satellites to tell accurately where it is.

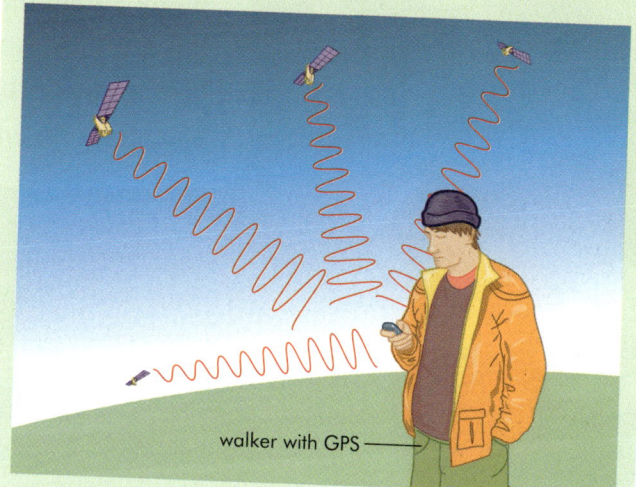

walker with GPS

- In what form does a GPS give its position? How is this useful?

- Describe one situation where someone might find a GPS useful.

- Explain in your own words why GPS satellites include the time in the signals they send out.

- How many satellites does a GPS receiver need to 'see' to be able to work out its position? Why are there so many GPS satellites in orbit around the Earth?

Activities

- Are there any activities you do, or would like to do, where a GPS might be useful? Discuss what they are and how a GPS could help you.

- Draw diagrams to show how knowing the distance to one place gives you a whole circle of places you could be in, knowing the distance to two places gives you only two places you could be in, and knowing the distance to three places lets you work out exactly where you are.

Space junk

Setting the scene

We hear about satellites all the time; you have probably heard about satellite television, satellite telephone communications, satellite navigation and research satellites. But how many satellites are there around the Earth, how big are they, how long have they been there, how many of them still work, and what do scientists do with them when they are broken?

Question: *How many satellites are there orbiting Earth?*

Answer: The first artificial satellite, Sputnik 1, was launched by the Russians in 1957. Since then, over 4800 satellites have been launched. Some of these have fallen back down to Earth, but there are still over 3500 satellites orbiting Earth.

Question: *How big are satellites?*

Answer: Satellites come in a huge range of sizes and weights. The first American satellite launched was only 2 metres long and weighed about 8 kilograms, but one of NASA's scientific Observatory satellites, launched in 1991, is over 21 metres across and weighs over 17 tonnes. Modern satellites tend to be smaller because they are cheaper to build and to launch into space. Many communications satellites weigh less than 100 kilograms; one space technology company has a set of 35 global tracking satellites weighing only 40 kilograms each, that's about the weight of a large dog.

Question: *How long do satellites stay working for?*

Answer: It depends on the satellite. Two things can stop a satellite working; it falls back down to Earth, or the equipment on board stops working. The closer to Earth a satellite is, the faster it falls out of orbit because the thicker atmosphere nearer Earth slows a satellite down more; a satellite 200 kilometres above the Earth's surface will only stay in orbit for a month or two, but one 1000 kilometres above the Earth's surface may stay in orbit for thousands of years. Satellites that have to orbit near Earth have booster rockets to keep moving them back out to where they should be, but most satellites only carry enough fuel for the rocket for about 10 years.

Question: *What is space junk, and why do scientists worry about it?*

Answer: Space doesn't have any rubbish bins. When satellites stop working or fall apart they just keep on orbiting and falling slowly towards Earth. Space junk is all the bits of artificial debris that is orbiting Earth. Over 25 000 bits of space junk have been catalogued, and there are at least 8000 bits still in orbit. They range from astronauts' gloves and screwdrivers to large chunks of rocket. Scientists need to know where they all are so that working satellites don't collide with them. The orbiting space junk can be moving at 27 000 kph, and at that speed even a small screwdriver could destroy a Space Shuttle and kill all the astronauts on board.

Question: *How can we get rid of space junk?*

Answer: In the past we couldn't, but now scientists are testing two ideas, which both use a long tether several kilometres long. In the first design, the tether latches onto a piece of space junk and acts like a brake to slow it down, so it falls out of orbit. In the second idea the tether swings round and round an orbiting mass. As it swings round, the tether catches a piece of space junk and flings it out to a higher orbit. The space junk gains extra energy and the tether loses energy, falling to a lower orbit, but the tether then uses solar energy to boost it back up to its original orbit to catch another piece of space junk. Scientists hope to have one of these ideas working successfully by 2010.

Qs

- How many satellites are there orbiting the Earth?

- Explain why low-orbit satellites do not stay in orbit for ever.

- Explain how there can be over 8000 bits of space junk in orbit when less than 5000 satellites have ever been launched.

- Explain, using diagrams if you wish, where the energy comes from to move a piece of space junk to a higher orbit using a tether.

Activities

- Satellites are now becoming much cheaper; cheap enough that poor developing countries can often afford to launch a satellite to monitor weather changes, for example. Discuss how a poor country might be able to benefit from this, and decide, as a group, whether you think it is a good way for them to spend money.

- Do some research about artificial satellites. Find out about one of the things they are used for and how it works. Explain what you have found out to the rest of your group, or class.

Faster than a speeding bullet

How fast is a train? If you've ridden on an old fashioned steam train or on a commuter train stopping at every station, you probably think trains are slow and noisy, but all round the world they are getting faster and faster. Find out about a train that people say is more like flying than going by train, and see why trains in Britain aren't that fast.

Setting the scene

The very first trains

The very first trains were steam trains, but much smaller than the steam trains you might have ridden on. The first train was built by an Englishman called Robert Trevithick in 1804. It pulled trucks full of iron and it went at about 7 kph, that's about a slow jogging pace. The first passenger train, in 1825, went at about 14 kph. Some people were really worried that the trains were getting faster; they said that if they went at 30 mph (48 kph) all the passengers would die because they wouldn't be able to breathe!

Getting faster – 'bullet trains'

By the 1960s nearly all trains in Britain had diesel engines instead of steam engines. They were much faster. The Intercity 125 trains, built in the 1970s, had a top speed of 125 mph (200 kph). All around the world, engineers worked at making trains even faster. They made engines more powerful, and the trains lighter, and they changed the shape of the front

of the train to make it as streamlined as possible. In 2004, South Korea started a 'bullet' train service, with trains that go at 300 kph (185 mph).

Magnetic levitation trains

In 2003, China opened the world's fastest passenger railway line, with a magnetic levitation train that went at 500 kph (310 mph) in test journeys. 'It's just like flying' said one delighted passenger. The magnetic levitation train is so fast because it doesn't have any friction at all. Very powerful electromagnets on the train and the track repel each other, so the whole train hovers about one centimetre above the track. Other magnets make the train go and stop. There are no surfaces rubbing against each other, so no friction.

Why don't trains in Britain go that fast?

As a train goes along, it bumps over all the joints where lengths of metal railway track have been joined together. If you listen to a train going past, you will hear the clattering as the wheels bump over the joints. The faster a train goes, the harder it bumps against all the joints. A really fast train needs a really strong, smooth railway track so that the pieces of railway track don't fall apart when the train bumps over them. Most of the railway lines in Britain were built many years ago when trains were much slower, so they are not strong enough for trains to go over them really fast. The old track is gradually being replaced with newer, stronger track, but it takes a long time and costs a lot of money. We can't use magnetic levitation trains either, because they need special tracks that are different from the ordinary railway lines.

These workers have to check the joints on the track regularly to make sure they are not going to break.

Qs

- How fast did the first passenger train go?

- Describe three changes engineers made to Intercity 125 trains to make them faster.

- Why is the magnetic levitation train so fast?

- If 'bullet' trains ran in Britain they would have to drive quite slowly. Explain why.

Activities

- 'Bullet' trains and magnetic levitation trains have advantages, but it would be expensive to change our railways to cope with these trains. Discuss whether or not you think it would be worth doing.

- Design an eye-catching poster to go in a travel agent's window to tell people about travelling either by 'bullet' train or by magnetic levitation train.

Magic mushrooms

You know that when the wind blows it exerts a force on things. It can blow them along or even blow them over. The faster the wind, the bigger the force. This can cause real problems for some buildings. Our interviewer talks to architect Elsa Lund to find out why the wind exerts a force on things, what buildings are affected most and what can be done about it.

Setting the scene

The top of this building may move backwards and forwards several metres in a strong wind. It's quite safe, but it feels uncomfortable.

Interviewer Good afternoon, Elsa. I've been told you work designing buildings that are more pleasant to be in when it is really windy.

Elsa Yes, that's right. Most really tall buildings can be uncomfortable places when it is windy because they sway. It even makes some people feel sick.

Interviewer That sounds very unpleasant, but why does the wind make them sway?

Elsa Wind is really just air particles moving along. As the air particles hit something they exert a force on it. The faster the wind, the faster the air particles are going when they hit a building, so the bigger the force they exert.

Interviewer So why is it only tall buildings that are affected by the wind?

Elsa It isn't, all buildings are affected, but you only notice it in tall buildings. The force on them is bigger because they have a bigger area for the wind to hit, and the wind gets stronger as you go higher into the air. The tops of tall buildings can move backwards and forwards by several metres; shorter buildings don't move anything like so far and people don't notice it.

Interviewer Tell us how you stop buildings swaying dangerously like this.

Elsa It's not dangerous. The metal frame inside can actually bend slightly in the wind, just as trees do. It doesn't do any harm. We only try to stop it because people in the buildings find it scary and uncomfortable.

Interviewer So what do you do?

Elsa We build in extra horizontal and diagonal beams to make the building more rigid. In really tall buildings we put in something called a 'wind compensating damper system'.

A computer system measures how much the wind is moving the building, and moves a heavy concrete weight, weighing several hundred tonnes, in the opposite direction, like a huge counterbalance weight. The computer system keeps moving the weight to keep the building balanced and still.

Interviewer Gosh, that sounds complicated. Isn't there an easier way?

Elsa Well, recently we have discovered that we can stick large mushroom shaped objects on the building to decrease its wind resistance.

Interviewer Hang on, that doesn't make sense. Surely sticking things on it will make the building less streamlined?

Will all tall buildings look like this one day, to prevent them being damaged by the wind?

Elsa You'd think so, wouldn't you? But actually the smooth shape of the 'mushroom' makes it easier for the wind to flow round the sides of the building instead of hitting straight into it. We've found that the best size 'mushroom' is about one-quarter to one-half the diameter of the building, with the 'mushrooms' placed about six times the diameter of the 'mushroom' apart.

Interviewer That must look really weird!

Elsa It does, but it stops a lot of wind damage to buildings, and makes them more comfortable to work in, and that's what really counts.

- Why does a strong wind make a building sway more than a gentle wind does?

- Is it dangerous when buildings sway in the wind? Why do architects try to design buildings that don't sway?

- Explain briefly in your own words how a 'wind compensating damper system' works.

- Why do 'mushrooms' on buildings work, even though they look as though they would make a building less streamlined?

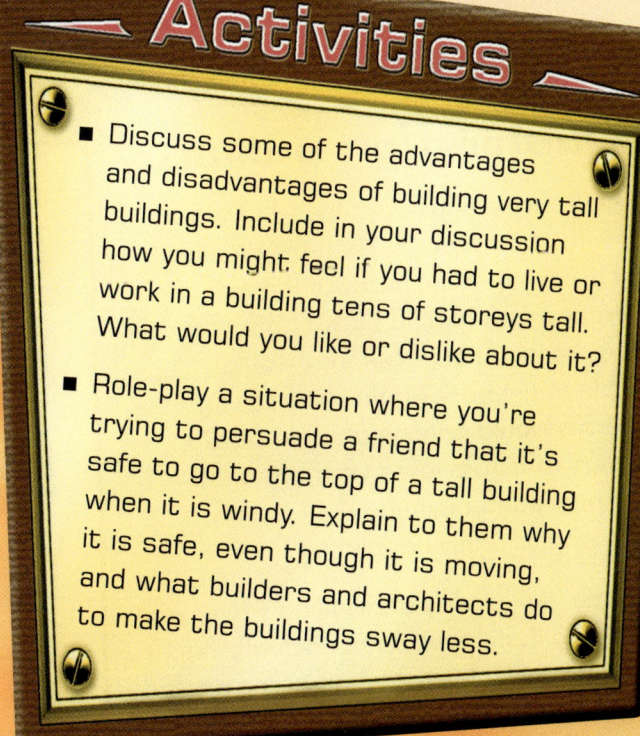

Activities

- Discuss some of the advantages and disadvantages of building very tall buildings. Include in your discussion how you might feel if you had to live or work in a building tens of storeys tall. What would you like or dislike about it?

- Role-play a situation where you're trying to persuade a friend that it's safe to go to the top of a tall building when it is windy. Explain to them why it is safe, even though it is moving, and what builders and architects do to make the buildings sway less.

We are sailing

In 1572, it took Francis Drake 25 days to sail across the Atlantic, yet the modern sailing record is less than 5 days, so why are boats so much quicker today? Francis Drake crossed the Atlantic from east to west with the 'trade winds' blowing from behind him, but modern record-breaking attempts are usually done from west to east, into the prevailing winds, so how is that faster, or even possible?

Forces and resistance

Any sailing boat has two sets of forces acting on it, forward forces from the wind tending to make it speed up and air resistance and water resistance tending to make it slow down. Modern sailing boats have much less water resistance than Drake's boats did. They are usually made from smooth fibreglass, painted with antifouling paints to prevent the growth of barnacles that would increase resistance. Modern hulls are much narrower for their length than older hulls, and they also have very deep keels, which give stability without increasing water resistance. Many modern sailing boats are catamarans or trimarans; they have two or three very narrow hulls side by side, which gives the stability of a very wide hull for only the resistance of a narrow hull.

Pushing or pulling?

At first everyone thinks the wind blows sailing boats along. Then they realise this can't be true, because if it was, the 'trade winds' would blow boats one way across the Atlantic but they wouldn't be able to get back again! Also sailing yachts would only be able to sail along rivers or across lakes when the wind happened to be in the right direction. So what is really happening?

If you look closely at a sailing yacht, you will see that the sail is not actually flat; it is curved like the top of an aeroplane's wing. As the wind blows across the

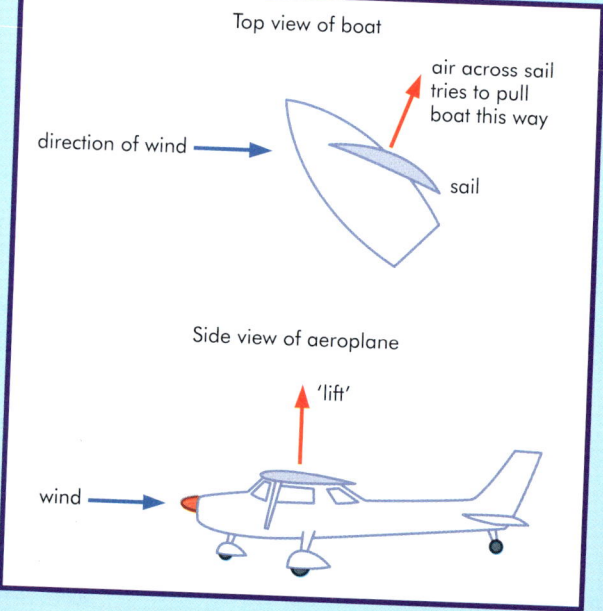

Top view of boat

air across sail tries to pull boat this way

direction of wind

sail

Side view of aeroplane

'lift'

wind

curved surface of the sail it acts exactly like an aeroplane wing, producing a force (the equivalent of 'lift' for an aeroplane) that pulls the sail, and the boat, in the direction of the curve of the sail. The force of the keel on the water stops the sideways effect of the force from the sail, so the boat moves forward, almost into the direction the wind is coming from.

Modern boats have hulls, masts, spars, rigging and sails that are being made from stronger and stronger materials, so modern boats can sail into stronger and stronger winds without damage, increasing the force on the boat and increasing the speed it can go at.

Tacking

You have probably heard accounts of boats being 'blown off course'. This is misleading because it makes it sound as if the wind is pushing the boat from behind, but it isn't. It is to do with the 'aeroplane wing' effect of the sail again. Because the wind has to blow across the surface of the sail, it is not possible to sail exactly into the wind (the forces would be trying to pull the boat sideways if you tried it). So if sailors want to sail directly into the wind they 'tack' to prevent their boat being 'blown off course'. They sail as 'close to the wind' as they can for a while, change tack and sail close to the wind on the other side. The boat moves in a zig-zag path but the overall effect is to sail towards the direction the wind is coming from.

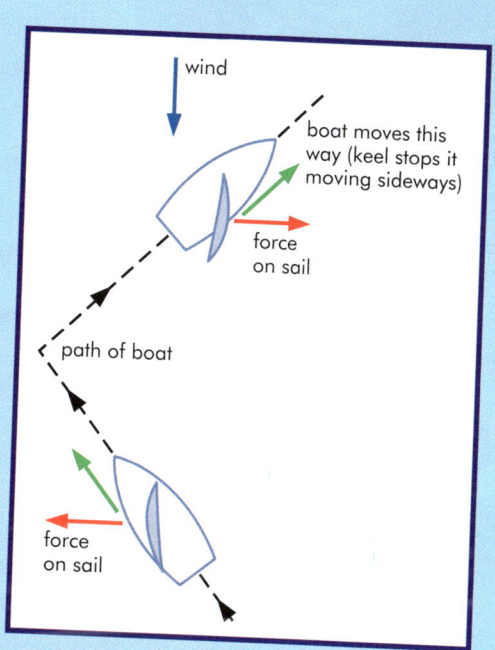

wind

boat moves this way (keel stops it moving sideways)

force on sail

path of boat

force on sail

Qs

- List three things that decrease the water resistance of modern sailing boats.

- Describe one piece of evidence that shows that sailing boats are not 'blown along by the wind'.

- Explain one similarity and one difference between a sail and an aeroplane wing.

- Explain, with reasons, why a sailing yacht would not be able to sail towards the wind along a very narrow canal or river.

Activities

- Imagine you were trying to teach someone how a sailing boat can steer. What would you say to them?

- Find out some more about 'Round-the-World' yachtsmen and women. Perhaps you could find the answers to some of these questions: What route do they usually take, and why? What type of boats do they use? What materials are the boats built from? What weather do they like best? What weather conditions/sailing skills give the fastest sailing times?

Take a deep breath

Getting the scene

Have you ever seen pictures on television of people scuba diving or snorkelling? You may even have seen underwater photographs of coral reefs or the seabed. It's like a whole new world waiting to be explored – but it's really hard to explore here. There are lots of problems that make exploring underwater really difficult and dangerous. We asked Bob, an expert underwater cameraman, to explain some of them.

Getting down, getting back up

Getting underwater is easy – you just jump in with heavy weights on your feet! Getting back up again is much harder. Divers usually go down from a boat and people in the boat pull them back up again when they are ready, but that wouldn't work for submarines. They have special tanks, called 'ballast tanks' that they fill with sea water when they want to go down, and fill with air, from tanks of compressed, liquid air, when they want to float back up again. When the air expands it makes the submarine light for its size, so it floats.

Getting suffocated

We need air to breathe – we can't get the oxygen we need underwater. Divers take a tank of air down with them and they have to remember to come back up before the tank is empty. The first submarines worked in the same way, but their tanks of air were bigger. Modern submarines can stay underwater for months because they use special chemicals to change the carbon dioxide we breathe out into carbon and oxygen.

Getting lost

As you go deeper underwater, it gets darker. A few tens of metres down it is pitch black, and very easy to get lost. Divers are usually tied to buoys or to boats on the surface, so they can follow the cable back to the boat. Most navigation systems don't work underwater, so submarines have to keep surfacing every few days to work out exactly where they are. While they are underwater they can use sonar (you might have heard a submarine's sonar 'pinging' on films) to tell where the seabed, rocks, boats or other submarines are.

Getting squashed

When you stand on Earth you have a column of air pushing down on top of you, but you can't feel it because you are so used to it. When you go underwater, you have lots of water pushing down on you as well, and water is heavy. If you go 10 metres down it is like having a 300 kilogram weight resting on your head, with another 300 kilograms added for every extra 10 metres you go down! That's partly why divers can't go very deep – they would get squashed. Submarines can go deeper, but they have to be round in shape because round shapes are very strong and the weight of water pushing down on them doesn't break them.

Getting the bends

Divers who go deeper than about 30 metres can suffer a problem called 'the bends' if they are not very careful. As they go deep underwater, the high pressure makes nitrogen gas, one of the gases in the air we breathe, dissolve into their blood. This doesn't matter if they surface slowly, because the nitrogen gas just slowly comes out of their blood again. If they surface too quickly, the nitrogen gas fizzes out of their blood suddenly, just like gas fizzing out of a bottle of cola when you open it. This makes the diver feel very ill, and it can even kill them. People in submarines don't have this problem. This is because the pressure inside the submarine is kept the same as the pressure at the surface, so the nitrogen doesn't dissolve into the submarine crew's blood.

Qs

- List the five problems scientists had to solve before they could dive deep underwater.

- Explain why divers cannot stay underwater for very long.

- How do modern submarines stay underwater for months at a time?

- Why is it easy to get lost underwater? How can submarines tell what is around them?

- Imagine you are 20 metres underwater. Work out the weight of water resting on your head.

Activities

- Imagine you are a diving instructor. Role-play explaining to your partner, who has never done any diving, about the dangers and how to stay safe. Then swap roles.

- Do some research. Find out some more about submarines; perhaps who uses them, and what for, what they are like and how they have changed. Find some pictures. Make a poster or scrapbook.

Cow power?

Setting the scene

You know that liquids are incompressible; you can't squash them. If you push hard on a container of liquid, the liquid has to go somewhere. You have probably seen this 'in action' in hypodermic syringes or in water pistols. It is also used in hydraulic systems, to put on car brakes when the driver pushes the brake pedal, for example. Now it is being used in poor countries to improve people's lifestyles.

The worst drought in decades

SCIENTISTS FEAR THAT SOME AREAS OF EASTERN AFRICA MAY BE FACING THEIR WORST DROUGHT FOR YEARS. 'The annual rains just haven't been heavy enough,' one aid worker told our reporter, 'fields are drying out and crops are dying,' she went on, 'people use water from the river to irrigate their fields, but water levels in the river are falling. Anyway the people have to lift all the water out of the river in buckets because they don't have any pumps, and they cannot really get enough water from the river to make a difference.'

'Thank you' say Ethiopian villagers

Thanks to our readers' generosity we have been able to install six new irrigation pumps in the village we told you about last month. 'We are so grateful,' said a spokesman for the village, 'now we can water our fields, so we can be sure of a harvest to feed our children. We even hope to grow some cash crops to sell, so we can buy ourselves more pumps for next year.'

The pumps are a low-cost, low-maintenance, new design from a company in New York. Each pump is made from a water-filled plastic bladder, with a metal plate over it. The pumps are fitted in the ground on paths that the village cattle use when they go to the river to drink. As a cow steps on the metal plate, it squashes the plastic bladder, forcing water out through a one-way valve. As the cow steps off the plate, springs make the bladder expand again, drawing water in through a second one-way valve. So all the time the cattle are thirsty, they are watering the fields as well!

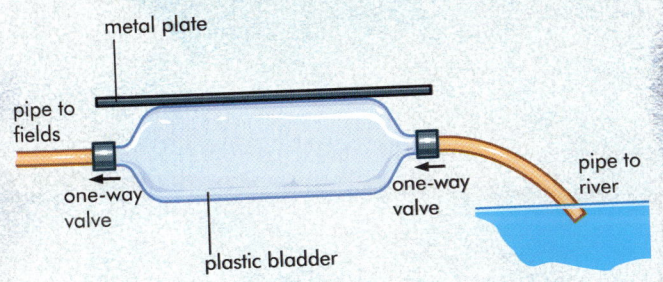

metal plate

pipe to fields

one-way valve

plastic bladder

one-way valve

pipe to river

THINGS ARE REALLY LOOKING UP!

DO YOU REMEMBER THE COW-POWER WATER PUMPS WE TOLD YOU ABOUT? The inventor says they could probably be used to generate electricity for poorer communities, as well as watering fields. 'We just need to alter the design a little,' a company spokesman told us, 'so that the water coming out of the bladder is used to turn round an electricity generator to generate electricity.' At present the company is trying out a design for use in small towns. Cars driving over the metal plate force water out of the pump to turn a generator, and then the water is returned to the pump to be pumped round again. 'It would certainly be possible to use the pump to water crops as well as generate electricity. The water would just flow onto the fields after it had turned the generator, instead of flowing back to the pump.' So hopefully it will not be too long before there is a small generator driven by cow or person power!

Qs

- What does 'irrigate' mean?

- Describe in your own words how the 'cow-power' pump works. You can include diagrams if you wish.

- Suggest how the amount of electricity generated might be related to the number of cars driving over the pump.

- Do you think the designers would have to make any changes to the pump, to make it suitable for use with cars, rather than with cows?

Activities

- Discuss the benefits that being able to water their crops, and possibly having a small supply of electricity, might bring to a poor African village.

- Can you think of anywhere else where this water-filled pressure-powered pump might be useful, or might save money and energy resources, possibly in your society? Discuss your ideas. You could even include a sketch to show how you would use the pump.

It balances!

You probably played on see-saws when you were tiny, and found that you get the best ride if you sit in the right place, so the weight each side of the see-saw is balanced. Now you know that it is actually the turning effects of the forces on each side of the pivot that must balance. Our expert explains how engineers can use this effect to create useful and spectacular bridges.

The raisable Saltina Bridge

In 1993, the town of Brig, near the Swiss Alps, suffered devastating damage when there was a flash flood on the nearby River Rhone. A bridge across the River Rhone trapped debris being carried downstream by the flooded river, blocking the path of the floodwater and causing many tonnes of floodwater, carrying boulders the size of cars, to rush through the town. Engineers wanted to make sure that such a disaster couldn't happen again. They couldn't remove the bridge across the Rhone – it was needed – but perhaps they could make it move out of the way when the river flooded. The answer they chose was to use the idea of a pivot and a counterweight, an idea that had been used in small bridges across canals in Britain for hundreds of years.

Can you see the counterweight balancing the turning effect of the bridge? Pulling down on a rope attached to the end of the 'top arm' makes the bridge lift up.

The 'Saltina' Bridge uses a pivot and a counterweight on a massive scale. The steel bridge itself weighs 152 tonnes, and it is pivoted at one end. On the other side of the pivot is a steel water container that can hold 50 m³ of water. Normally the turning effect of the bridge is greater than the turning effect of the water container, and the bridge rests in place across the river. When the water level in the river rises high enough, water flows into the water container, filling it and making the turning effect on that side of the pivot greater. The bridge tips up, allowing floodwater to flow harmlessly down the river. It takes just five minutes for the water container to fill and the bridge to lift. The bridge can only be lowered again when the river level falls, by pumping the water out of the container.

The Gateshead Millennium Bridge

In 1997, a competition was held to design a new bridge to carry pedestrians and cyclists across the River Tyne at Gateshead, near Newcastle in the north-east of England. The bridge had to open to allow a clear channel at least 30 metres wide for large ships to pass through, with at least 25 metres of 'headroom'. The people of Gateshead voted for the winning design, and the bridge opened in September 2001. It has become famous worldwide as the world's first tilting bridge, often called the 'Blinking Eye' bridge, as people say it looks like an eye blinking as it opens.

The Gateshead Millennium Bridge is made from two arches, one forming the walkway and cycleway across the river, the other arch supporting it. The bridge is pivoted on two supports, one on each bank of the river, and when it opens it simply rotates around the pivot. The bridge spans a total distance of 126 metres across the river, weighs more than 850 tonnes and contains enough steel to make about 64 double-decker buses! Eight electric motors open the bridge, which is so well balanced that it takes just four minutes to open and costs just a few pounds. The bridge even cleans up its own litter; as the bridge opens, any litter dropped on the walkway or cycleway rolls into special traps at each end of the bridge.

Qs

○ Why did the town of Brig suffer flooding in 1993?

○ Draw a labelled diagram to show the bridge, the pivot and the water container for the Saltina Bridge.

○ If the water container for the Saltina Bridge was larger it could be placed closer to the pivot of the bridge. Describe one advantage and one disadvantage this would have for building and operating the bridge.

○ Suggest what might happen to the Gateshead Millennium Bridge if the turning effect of the supporting arch was greater than the turning effect of the walkway and cycleway.

Activities

- The Gateshead Millennium Bridge is so spectacular that it has become a real tourist attraction. Imagine you are on Gateshead town council and discuss what to do with all the tourists. Will you try to discourage them, or perhaps open and shut the bridge for their entertainment and charge them to go across it?

- Design a toy, useful device or ornament that uses tilting and balancing. Explain to a partner how your design works.

Acknowledgements

The author and publishers would like to thank the following for providing photographs.

Alamy: Travel-Shots 37;
AP: Katsumi Kasahara 46;
Corbis: Adam Woolfitt 41, Hulton-Deutsch Collection 34;
Corel 11 (NT): 48;
Corel 178 (NT): 47;
Corel 556 (NT): 70;
Corel 584 (NT): 68;
Digital Vision 9 (NT): 54;
Jeff Heads: 79 top, bottom;
NASA: JIC 52;
Natural World: 44;
Photodisc 54 (NT): 66;
Roslin Institute: 12;
Science Photolibrary: Pascal Goetcheluck 10, St Bartholomew's
   Hospital 19;
UNESCO: 33.

Picture research by John Bailey